Understanding Economic Growth

Jati Sengupta

Understanding Economic Growth

Modern Theory and Experience

Springer

Jati Sengupta
University of California, Santa Barbara
College of Letters & Science
Dept. Economics
North Hall 2024
Santa Barbara, California 93106-9210
jatisengupta@yahoo.com

ISBN 978-1-4419-8025-0 e-ISBN 978-1-4419-8026-7
DOI 10.1007/978-1-4419-8026-7
Springer New York Dordrecht Heidelberg London

Printed on acid-free paper

Springer is part of Springer Science+Business Media (www.springer.com)

Once I asked my dad: How should I lead my life?
He replied: Life is a dream, make it real.
I asked my mom the same question.
Came the reply: God overhead, heart within.
I dedicate this volume to my parents for all they taught me in life.

–Jati Sengupta

Preface

Modern economies today have undergone a dramatic change. There has been a shift from large-scale material manufacturing to the design and application of new technology with R&D and human capital. The new information age has introduced significant productivity gains through increasing returns and learning by doing. This has challenged the traditional growth models based on competitive market structures. Institutions outside the traditional markets and the genetic principle of survival of the fittest have dominated the current theory of industry growth. This volume coordinates and integrates the two strands of economic growth and development: the endogenous theory of growth and the extra-market models of evolutionary economics dominated by innovation efficiency.

A systematic treatment of the new paradigms of growth and development is attempted in this volume. The discussion is nonmathematical and nontechnical but analytic and synthetic. New paradigms of growth theory today have emphasized three basic features of endogenous growth: technology and innovations, institutions and extra-market dynamics, and core competence of evolutionary dynamics. This volume presents this new paradigm in terms of both theory and historical experiences.

Four key features of this volume are: role of innovations and human capital, impact of information technology, institutions as mechanisms of evolutionary economies, and the experiences of Asian growth miracles. Two extra-market forces are discussed here in some detail. One is the dynamic role of institutions and agencies of governance, which can reduce the large transaction costs and facilitate economic change. The second is the view of economic growth as an evolutionary process, where dynamic flexibility and creative competence play crucial roles. Traditional economic theory of growth has neglected these institutional and evolutionary systems of economic change. The present volume integrates the endogenous growth theory with the evolutionary models of economic change.

We attempt here a synthesis of modern economic theory of growth and recent models of evolutionary economics, which emphasizes the structural process of development. Growth and development complete the two phases: one complements the other.

The volume developed out of my long research in the area of economic growth and development. The microtheoretic foundations of economic growth are integrated here with the macroscopic foundations of economic change. Here nonmarket institutions play roles as important as the capitalistic markets. The new innovations disrupt the traditional static equilibria and bring new profits, which then augment further innovations. Growth is viewed as a cumulative process. The miracles can be repeated. The mantra is to learn, coordinate, and integrate.

Santa Barbara, CA Jati Sengupta

Contents

Chapter 1
Development

How does a nation grow? What causes development? This is the basic question economists attempted to answer since 1776, when Adam Smith published the volume: *An Inquiry into the Nature and Causes of the Wealth of Nations*. Since then the theory on economic development has moved forward from the classical and neoclassical to modern schools. On the empirical side we have now available diverse cross-section data of a significant number of countries, which provide a global picture of the process of development.

Excluding the oil-rich countries economic development has followed diverse trends over time for different countries. The cross-section data of real income in these countries reveal some important characteristics of the development process.

One of the most important conclusions of modern growth theory in economics is that capital investment is key to economic growth measured in terms of real income. The Harrod–Domar model predicts this trend, and if we include both physical and human capital in the composite concept of capital, then it yields the central hypothesis of modern endogenous growth models, where it is called AK model in one variant. The AK model is called so due to the linear production model Y = AK, where Y is real output, K is composite capital, and A reflects the technology. This production function exhibits constant returns to scale. This simple AK model of endogenous growth predicts that permanent (long-run) changes in capital investment rates should lead to permanent changes in a country's growth of gross domestic product (GDP) per capita. Jones (1995) tested this central hypothesis of the AK model for 15 OECD countries over the period 1950–1938 and found no empirical evidence of this hypothesis.

> In fact growth rates of GDP per capita show little or no persistent increases in the post-World War II era for OECD economies; what change has occurred is down rather than up. Two possibilities are suggested: either by some astonishing coincidence all of the movements in variables that can have permanent effects on growth have been offsetting, or the hallmark of the endogenous growth models, that permanent changes in policy variables have permanent effects on growth rates, is misleading (Jones 1995).

A second stylized fact is the East Asian miracle. Lucas (1993) called it a growth miracle and suggested policies for making such miracles. East Asia has a remarkable record of high and sustained economic growth. From 1965 to 1990 its 23 economies

J. Sengupta, *Understanding Economic Growth: Modern Theory and Experience*,
DOI 10.1007/978-1-4419-8026-7_1, © Springer Science+Business Media, LLC 2011

grew faster than those of all other regions. Most of the achievement is attributed by a World Bank study to the seemingly miraculous growth in just eight high-performing Asian economies, e.g., Japan, the four tigers: Hong Kong, South Korea, Singapore, and Taiwan, and the three newly industrialized countries (NICs) of Southeast Asia: Indonesia, Malaysia, and Thailand. The average growth rates of GDP per capita over the period 1968–1998 are 6.9 for China, 6.7 for Taiwan, 6.6 for South Korea, 6.0 for Singapore, and 4.9 for Indonesia. This may be compared to 2.6 for India, 2.0 for Brazil, and 0.2 for Argentina. For the last 3 years, China's GDP growth rates exceeded 10%, whereas the USA achieved less than 4.5%. What are the causes of the remarkable growth episode of the NICs in Asia?

A third stylized fact is the widening gap between rich and poor countries of the world. Helpman (2004) has termed it as one of the mysteries of economic growth. In 1960 there was a bunching of regions, with East Asia and the Pacific, South Asia, the sub-Saharan Africa, and the less-developed countries (LDCs) having an average per capita income around 1/9 to 1/10 of that in high-income OECD countries. Helpman has noted an important reason for the widening of the gap.

> It is encouraging how much less-developed countries benefit from R&D in the industrial countries. These benefits are even larger when measured in consumption rather than GDP units, because larger levels of R&D in the industrial countries bring about terms-of-trade improvements in the less-developed countries. Nevertheless, these results also have a discouraging side: they show that investment in innovation widens the gap between rich and poor countries. The output gains of the industrial countries exceed the output gains of the less-developed countries. We therefore conclude that investment in innovation in the industrialized countries leads to divergence of income between the North and the South (Helpman 2004).

Despite a reduction in the relative differences between many countries, absolute gaps in per capita income have increased according to the World Bank reports. Even for the NICs in Southeast Asia the absolute difference in income with high-income OECD countries widened from about $6,000 in 1960 to $13,000 in 1998 in terms of 1985 US dollars. The technology gap studies have shown that the domestic capability to absorb knowledge spillovers and R&D processes from abroad is a key factor in explaining growth rate differentials over the space between rich and poor countries.

Another important characteristic of the development process is income inequality. A World Bank study of 77 countries with 82% of the world's population shows that between the 1950s and the 1990s inequality rose in 45 of the countries and fell in 16. Latin-American and Caribbean countries have the world's highest income inequality. World inequality is very high. In 1993 the poorest 10% of the world's population had only 1.6% of the income of the richest.

The NICs of Southeast Asia have low Gini coefficients in the 30s, where Gini coefficient is a measure of inequality, high value indicating high inequality. China and India, the two countries with low but rapidly growing per capita incomes and large populations deserve some special mention. In China income inequality has followed a U-shaped pattern with inequality falling until the mid-1980s and rising since. The story is better in India with inequality falling until 2005 and then coming to a halt.

The high-income inequality places millions in extreme poverty and severely limits the benefits of equally shared growth for the poor. Inequality can augment the adverse effects of market and policy failures on economic growth. It is also likely to erode social capital including the sense of trust and citizen responsibility that is key to the sustainability of sound public institutions. Also, inequality undermines social support for high-quality universal public education, which is so crucial for increasing growth in LDCs. The empirical data on growth and development in the world shows enormous variation in per capita income across economies. Their rates of growth also vary enormously. According to the estimates by Jones (2002), it took 50 years to double the per capita GDP for the USA, but Japan did it in 16 years and Taiwan and South Korea did it in 12 years. The average annual growth rates over the period 1960–1997 were 1.4% for the USA, 4.4% in Japan, 5.6% in Taiwan, and 5.0% in South Korea, respectively. The per capita GDP in 1985 US dollars were $20,000 for the USA, $16,000 for Japan, $11,720 for Taiwan, and $10,131 for South Korea. Hong Kong and Singapore recorded $18,811 and $17,559 with average annual growth rates of 5.2 and 5.4%, respectively. How are we going to explain this wide diversity in growth and development patterns?

Economic theory attempts to explain the causes in terms of the production process, the market and the technology. But this is not sufficient, argues the institutional approach. The deep determinants are embedded in the various economic and social institutions, which set the rules of the game and provide operating rules of coordination and organizational efficiency. These rules are fundamental in the sense that they determine the organizational environment for production and exchange. The latter determines the success or failure of the optimizing economic rules of behavior.

The evolutionary approach goes one step further. It views development as a biological process of evolution, where both economic institutions and the production across the market system and the extraeconomic organizations like the legal framework imposed by government or the development of an incentive structure through patent laws for innovations. North (1990) emphasized most strongly that optimizing transaction costs along with production costs determine the rules of efficiency of an optimal economic and institutional order. With zero transaction costs the institutional choice problem does not arise. But the real world where optimizing economic rules would have to be applied, transaction costs are substantial. Hence, we need an institutional approach, which has to evolve through a process of learning by doing. As North points out:

> The evolution of institutions that create a hospitable environment for cooperative solutions to complex exchange provides for economic growth. The central focus here is on the problem of human cooperation, specifically the cooperation that permits economies to capture the gains from trade that were the key to Adam Smith's *Wealth of Nations*.
>
> There are two forces shaping the path of institutional change: increasing returns and imperfect markets characterized by significant transaction costs. In a world where there are no increasing returns to institutions and markets are competitive, institutions do not matter (North 1990).

The evolutionary growth models emphasize the structural dynamics of industry growth diffusion. Thus, organizational change is one aspect. The other aspects involve three main mechanisms that guide the process of industrial evolution:

1. A mechanism of diversity creation in the field of goods and services and technology
2. A mechanism of transmission of diversity to other sectors through backward and forward linkage, i.e., more input usage and more output demand
3. A mechanism of selection by which the successful firms on the innovations frontier emerge as leaders

New technology and innovations create a hypercompetitive world, where Schumpeterian competition plays a dynamic role. Schumpeter emphasized the twin forces of "creative destruction" and "creative accumulation" due to technological innovation, by which old firms and industries are continually replaced by new ones. Nelson and Winter (1982) viewed Schumpeterian competition as the standard model of industrial change, which yields the evolution of new industry structures. Anderson (1994) recently discussed Winter's work as follows:

> In Winter's work institutions played a role because he focused on the constant interaction between institutional properties of the technological trajectory and the learning activities of firms. Recent evolution theorists emphasized the theory of *interactive learning* as a source of diffusion. Learning is connected to innovation. It involves both the introduction of knowledge and the diffusion of knowledge in the form of products or processes. Learning leads to new knowledge and entrepreneurs of different kinds use this knowledge to form innovative ideas and projects. Diffusion and learning processes are inseparable and mutually reinforcing (Anderson 1994).

1.1 Economic Growth

The terms "development" and "growth" are often used as synonyms. In economic literature the theory of economic development has been mostly concerned with the process by which an underdeveloped country achieves a development stage. It attempts to explain the process of increase in income and level of living. It is sometimes called the *level effect*. Economic growth theory is usually applied for explaining the steady-state or long-run growth measured by the percentage increase in national income or some measure of the standard of living such as the human development index (HDI). This is sometimes called the *growth effect*, which was employed by Solow (1956) to emphasize the dynamic role of technological progress. Real per capita income is often used to measure economic development or growth. The "real" part refers to two adjustments made to the monetary income, i.e., price fluctuations and foreign exchange fluctuations. The latter is based on PPP (purchasing power parity) theory, which allows to measure the real worth of income from exports. The real income measure is based on the GDP as the sum total of all goods and services produced by the economy in a year. This measure, however, ignores two deep determinants of economic development. The first is the contribution of human development. This is remedied by a measure called HDI by the United Nations Development Program (UNDP). The HDI is a composite measure, which combines real income, life expectancy, and educational level. The second aspect ignored in the income measure is the transaction costs and benefits associated with the given institutional structure of the economy. This has been strongly emphasized by the recent institutional and evolutionary schools.

The long-term growth experience of fast-growing and slow-growing countries reveals an interesting pattern. The following data from Pasinetti and Solow (1994) provide cross-country averages (1960–1989) for 12 fast-growing and 15 slow-growing countries (mean per capita growth rate is 1.92).

	Fast growers	Slow growers
Share of investment in GDP	0.27	0.17
Education		
Secondary school enrollment	0.27	0.07
Primary school enrollment	0.90	0.52
Govt expenditure/GDP	0.14	0.13
Inflation rate (%)	8.42	16.51
Black market exchange rate premium	4.65	75.03
Share of exports in GDP	0.44	0.29

Two interesting points emerge from this data. The first is that the investment rate, education, and exports are much higher for the fast growers. Second, the market distortions measured by the inflation rate and the black market exchange rate premium are much lower for the faster growers. This empirical experience agrees very well with the modern growth theory in economics.

Recent developments in economic growth theory have started with Solow's formulation of neoclassical theory. Aggregate savings, he argued, finance investment as additions to the national capital stock. An economy with an initially low capital–labor ratio will have a high marginal product of capital. Then if a constant proportion of income is saved, the gross investment in new capital goods may exceed the amount needed to offset depreciation. Over time capital per worker will rise, which with constant returns to scale and a fixed technology will generate a decline in the marginal product of capital. This decline will cause the savings generated by the income from new capital to also fall and eventually be only sufficient to cover depreciation. At this point the economy enters a stationary state with an unchanging standard of living. How could growth occur in the steady state? Solow offered two reasons. One is that the marginal product of capital remains above a certain positive level. The Harrod–Domar model precisely did this by assuming a linear production function with a fixed positive marginal product of capital. But the Solow model assumed a neoclassical production function where the marginal product of capital declines as more capital is employed. The other possibility is through a shift in the production frontier, which is called "technological progress." However, even in a world where technological progress provides the engine of long-run economic growth in income, accumulation of physical capital will play an independent role during the transitional phase. Technology, however, is assumed to be exogenous in the Solow model. It also ignores the contribution of human capital in the form of educational skills and the level of knowledge, e.g., R&D investments. On both counts the empirical evidence does not support Solow's hypothesis. For instance, lots of research studies on industrial innovations or technology in fields such as synthetic chemicals, semiconductors, and personal computers have shown that firms invested in these new technologies when they saw an opportunity to earn profits. The concept of technological progress in the Solow model was made endogenous by Lucas (1993) and Paul Romer (1994). Endogeneity is from intentional investment decisions made by entrepreneurs seeking to earn quasi-monopoly profits due to "first mover" advantages. Lucas (1993) introduced several new dimensions of endogenous technology. While emphasizing the point that the growth miracles in the newly industrializing countries (NICs) of Southeast Asia cannot in general be explained by physical capital accumulation alone, he discussed the role of human capital in schools and on the job. The rate of expansion of knowledge in both forms transforms a *level effect* into a *growth effect.*

1.2 Knowledge Capital

The knowledge capital takes several forms: R&D, on-the-job learning, research in applied and basic forms in public institutions such as universities and private industries, and general level of education in the economy from primary, secondary, and tertiary stages. The notion of knowledge capital is most important for economic growth for its "learning-by-doing" effect, a term first used by Arrow (1962) for explaining productivity growth in the aircraft industry. Learning has two types of impact. One is that it augments the total stock of design knowledge by increasing its efficiency. The other is that human capital employed in the R&D division of private industry generates an expansion of the stock of knowledge. It is generally subject to increasing returns, and it is complementary to all other inputs. Arrow pointed out that the productivity of human capital in both basic and applied research is an increasing function of the accumulated knowledge capital. As a result the cost of producing new designs declines over time.

An important dimension of new endogenous technology like software development is its spillover effect. Lucas has termed this learning spillover technology, which is considered as the source of rapid productivity growth and openness in external trade generating mutual gains from trade.

Spence (1984) has discussed in some detail the cost-reducing impact of R&D expenditures, which are largely fixed costs. These expenditures create externality problems leading to the so-called market failure. If the R&D for the single firm is not appropriable by itself, the initial incentives to do the R&D are reduced. On the other hand, the price of the R&D, namely, zero, is close to its marginal cost of transmitting it to other firms. The output of R&D has the character of a public good.

He argues that it is economically more preferable to supply the public good publicly or subsidize the private supplier without paying for the subsidy by charging the users on the basis of use.

Cost-reducing economies of scale differ from economies of learning by learning. The former refers to the ability to perform a production activity at a lower cost when it is performed on a larger scale at a particular point in time. But learning economies refers to the reduction in unit costs due to accumulating experience over time.

One has to note that the spillover technology is closely associated with the Schumpeterian concept of innovation in many forms, e.g., R&D, new processes, new products, and new markets. The market power is the key source of this innovation process. This generates more nonrival inputs and outputs through knowledge capital. In many ways the spillover technology allows dynamic externalities to generate dynamic gains from trade. Thus, declining computer prices and improved inputs have helped the NICs in Asia and China to achieve a faster rate of growth.

1.3 Concluding Remarks

Development and economic growth have been central to economic thought in recent years. The recent dynamics of industry growth, technology diffusion, and globalization have a dramatic impact on current economic growth of nations, significantly changing the market structure and world trade, and challenging the paradigm of competitive equilibrium and their guiding principles.

Two important phases of economic growth theory are characterized by technology and knowledge innovations. The development of computer industry and other high-tech industries today have intensified the market competition and innovation dynamics in the fast-growing countries like the NICs in Asia and China. Increasing efficiency and productivity growth have played a central role in industry growth in the fast-growing countries. The learning by doing, scale effects, and externalities have played most dynamic roles. The institutional and evolutionary theorists have emphasized the dynamic role of improved organization and educational structures. Thus, Winter (1984) focused on the constant interaction between the institutional properties of the technological trajectory and the learning activities of firms. Recent evolution theorists emphasized the process of *interactive learning* as the source of knowledge diffusion. Learning is closely connected to innovation. It involves both the introduction of knowledge in the form of goods and processes, e.g., software development, and also the provision of new incentives for improving the process through imitation and diffusion. Thus, diffusion and learning processes are inseparable and mutually reinforcing.

Chapter 2
The Market

The economic theory of markets has been central to economic growth since the days of Adam Smith. There have been three major phases of this theory: the classical theory, the neoclassical theory, and the modern theory of global markets. Adam Smith is the first classical economist who emphasized the role of markets in industry growth. His economic contribution *The Wealth of Nations* contains several features of the market evolution, which leads to industry growth and overall economic development.

Competition in private markets and the balancing of supply and demand in equilibrium are the first aspects identified by Adam Smith. He both identifies the tendency of competition toward equilibrium and implies that the allocation of resources thereby produced is optimal from society's point of view. This theory of economic equilibrium is intrinsically related to the theory of economic evolution. Technological progress for Smith is not an exogenous force affecting economic growth but central to his theory of economic development. As Richardson (1975) points out as follows:

> In *The Wealth of Nations* competition is given more to do than equate demands and supplies within the context of a given industrial structure and a given technology; the invisible hand has also to adapt both structure and technology to the fresh opportunities created by expanding markets. In our modern microeconomic theory, on the other hand, it is the equilibrating and allocative functions of competition that obtain all but exclusive attention; technical progress is made exogenous and structural evolution largely ignored.

2.1 The Classical Approach

Adam Smith laid great emphasis on increasing returns as a source of economic growth and development. He pointed out that the division of labor and specialization due to increasing returns leads to the establishment of new trades. But for this to happen the market has to be large enough. He stressed the gains from foreign trade, which help widen the extent of the market – thereby raising the productivity of the trading countries. Central to the gains from free trade are the allocative efficiency

J. Sengupta, *Understanding Economic Growth: Modern Theory and Experience*,
DOI 10.1007/978-1-4419-8026-7_2, © Springer Science+Business Media, LLC 2011

gains arising from international specialization based on absolute differences in costs. Trade enables a country to buy goods from abroad at a lower real cost than that at which they can be produced at home.

In modern growth theory Lucas (1993) and others have strongly emphasized the role of increasing returns through direct foreign investment, which induced learning by doing through knowledge capital. The newly industrialized countries (NICs) of Southeast Asia have achieved very high growth rates in the last two decades, and the export market had played a most dynamic role.

In recent decades the economies have undergone a profound transformation from large-scale material manufacturing to the design and use of new technologies depending on improved software and designs. These new technologies are increasingly characterized by increasing returns to scale. These are mechanisms of positive feedback that act to reinforce other complementary forces. These increasing returns occur due to three main reasons: (1) high fixed costs and very low variable costs, (2) network effects where the value of a product increases with the number of users, and (3) high switching costs.

2.2 The Neoclassical View

The neoclassical approach to economic growth has used two basic premises. The first is the competitive model of Walrasian equilibrium, where markets play a critical role in allocating resources efficiently. Markets for labor, capital, and finance following competitive rules help to secure the optimal allocation of inputs and outputs. This type of competitive paradigm was used by Solow to develop a growth model, which used a production function with labor and capital as substitutable inputs subject to diminishing returns. The second premise of the neoclassical model assumes that technology is given. Solow used the interpretation that the technology in the production function is exogenous. The point is that R&D investment and human capital through learning by doing were not explicitly recognized.

Solow used a Cobb–Douglas production function with two substitutable inputs: labor and capital, and a technology factor. While competitive market forces determine the allocation of labor and new capital, technology is assumed to be completely exogenous. With a constant saving–income ratio, an increase in aggregate capital stock helps initially to raise income, but as capital per worker rises, diminishing returns set in, generating a decline in the marginal product of capital. In the long run the economy enters a stationary steady state with unchanging standard of living. Despite this the neoclassical growth theorists were not pessimistic about the long-run prospects for the aggregate economy. This is because technological progress could shift the production frontier upward. Solow showed that with advances in technology, which he took to augment the labor productivity at an exogenous rule, the marginal product of capital need not decline as capital per worker increased.

The neoclassical emphasis on competitive markets and their role in allocating resources such as labor and capital optimally in a decentralized economy has received three types of challenges in recent times. First, the dynamics of high-technology industry growth in recent times have changed the market structure and world trade most dramatically. In the world of innovations in new technology and the spillover of R&D investment effects, various forms of noncompetitive market structures have evolved in recent times. Second, the endogenous growth models have recently emphasized the role of inputs such as human capital and R&D capital, which have significant spillover effects for other industries and other countries, and these may have either constant or increasing returns; also these inputs may be complementary rather than rivalrous to other inputs such as labor and physical capital. Also much of technology inventions in Solow's model is market driven, since firms have invested in new technologies when they see an opportunity to earn profits. Finally, one should note the cases of market failure, where competitive principles fail to perform their function. Then cases generate a divergence between the private and social optimum in resource allocations. In many markets, firms compete over time by cost-reducing investments. In many instances they take the form of developing new products with cheaper prices. Cost-reducing expenditures are largely fixed costs. In a market system the criterion for determining the value of cost-reducing R&D is profitability or revenues. Since revenues may understate the social benefits in the aggregate and at the margin, there is no reason to expect a competitive market to result in the optimal outcome. Furthermore, R&D largely represents fixed costs, and depending on the technological environment, sometimes a large one, market structures are likely to be concentrated and imperfectly competitive with consequences for prices and allocative efficiency. Also R&D expenditure has externality benefits and spillover effects on other firms. These effects reduce the incentives to perform R&D investments, creating a divergence between private and social optimum.

The neoclassical growth model developed by Solow fails to explain the most basic fact of actual growth behavior. To a large extent this failure is due to the model's prediction that per capita output approaches a steady state path along which it grows at a rate that is given exogenously. This means that the long-term rate of national growth is determined outside the model and is independent of preferences and most aspects of the production function and policy measures.

2.3 The Modern Approach

The modern approach to market dynamics has several basic features. First, the new economic order emerging today, sometimes called the new economy, is spreading all over the world. This is nothing short of an industrial revolution. It is a revolution in information explosion and in knowledge capital. Three key elements of this revolution are worth emphasizing: (1) increasing efficiency of the microcomputer industry and telecommunications, (2) interfirm and interindustry diffusion of knowledge, and (3) new innovations in the Schumpeterian sense and the global expansion of trade through network and market externalities. Economies of scale occur in market demand, which stimulates productivity of existing and improved inputs. Modern growth theory emphasizes two main channels of inducing growth through R&D expenditures, which include knowledge capital and the core component of knowledge innovations. One is the impact on the range of available goods and services and the other is its impact on the stock of knowledge and the so-called learning-by-doing phenomena. Helpman (2004) has discussed the role of endogenous R&D investments in improving industrial productivity of a developing country participating in world markets through international trade. Two impacts are distinguished. The first is the market size effect: this is very similar to Adam Smith's ideas. Access to a larger world market raises the probability of inventive activities and encourages more R&D investment and more knowledge creation. The second is the competitive effect, which has two sides. On the negative side, it may hurt profits in the short run, since foreign competitors are more efficient than domestic firms. On the positive side, however, open competition may induce the domestic technological leaders in business to forge ahead. The NICs of Southeast Asia such as South Korea, Taiwan, and Hong Kong and also Japan have adopted this positive side of competitive efficiency, and the openness in trade has opened up new challenges by which these countries achieved a very high growth rate in the last two decades.

An important feature of the modern approach to market dynamics is its view of the market as a set of social institutions in which a large number of commodity exchanges regularly take place, and to a large extent, these exchanges are facilitated and structured by those institutions.

2.4 The Institutional Approach

In the neoclassical market model the primary institutions that facilitate exchange are private ownership and legally enforceable contracts. Exchange is done through contracts, and the governments ensure compliance with contracts. But the neoclassical model does not reflect the breadth and complexity of behavior actually correlated in markets.

The institutional approach to market dynamics and economic growth has emphasized several important features for the theory of economic development. First, the institutions are rules or humanly devised constraints, which allow agents to form expectations about the behavior of other agents and thus facilitate coordination among them. Thus, the major role of institutions relating to markets and the various interindustry linkages is to reduce the various uncertainties arising from incomplete information about other agents' behavior by establishing a stable structure to human interactions. The three most important aspects of the role of institutions in securing an efficient market system are the transaction cost (TC) approach, the equilibrium-of-the-game approach (EG), and the evolutionary approach.

The TC approach is central to the new institutional approach. The neoclassical paradigm with competitive general equilibrium emphasizing efficiency in resource allocation is invalid in the word of positive transaction costs. Not only do positive transaction costs exist but also they are in fact quantitatively substantial. According to some estimates, transaction costs in modern market economies comprise as much as 50–60% of net national product. The discovery of transaction costs by Ronald Coase (1937) started a revolution in microeconomic thinking. Market transaction costs consist primarily of information and bargaining costs. These have three components: (1) search and information costs, (2) bargaining and decision costs, and (3) supervision and enforcement costs. The recent management science literature has emphasized the managerial transaction costs. In the neoclassical world all these transaction costs are ignored. It is important to refer to the Coase theorem here, as follows:

> Individuals who are normally only interested in maximizing their own incomes and not concerned with social cost will only undertake an activity if the value of the product of the factors employed is greater than their private costs. But if private cost is equal to social cost, it follows that the individuals will only engage in an activity if the value of the product of the factors employed is greater than the value which they would yield in their best alternative use. That is to say, with zero transaction costs, the value of production would be maximized (Coase 1998).

Three important implications of the Coase theorem are to be noted. The first is that the competitive general equilibrium solution is no longer efficient in a world of positive transaction costs. Market and other institutions turn out to be inefficient, and this inefficiency is basic and fundamental in the long run. Models of economic growth of the neoclassical school, which were utilized by Solow and other growth theorists, are, therefore, untenable to a large extent. Second, regulatory policies of government such as the FTC, which attempt to secure competitive efficiency without incorporating positive transaction costs, are not likely to be appropriate. Thus, the competitive model turns out to be a poor vehicle for understanding a wide variety of competitive tactics and institutions. Finally, the relationships between institutions and economic productivity are completely ignored. Economists almost take it for granted that modern economies need to be largely structured through markets and good institutions to support the effective operation of such an economy. But it is unclear what the effective operation of a market economy means. As Schumpeter argued long ago that the standard neoclassical theory of market organization and behavior is not capable of dealing with the phenomenon of innovation, which is so crucial to sustained economic growth. It is thus clear that once we emphasize the factors that support and speed up the innovation, a number of nonmarket organizations such as universities, public R&D research programs, and spillover effects turn out to be important along with the market organization. Thus, we need to develop a theory of innovation-driven economic growth that recognizes the key roles played by the nonmarket structures as well as those conventionally seen as market ones.

In many underdeveloped economies inefficient institutions inflate the share of transaction cost in the total cost of economic development to such an extent that growth is impeded and market failures including lack of coordination between market and nonmarket institutions generate significant inefficiency in resource allocation and economic productivity. As a result the divergence of private social costs and benefits increases to a significant degree. This is time for both infrastructure activity and other developmental expenditures such as public education and research activities.

While transaction cost adds a monetary dimension to total costs of growth and industrialization, the EG (equilibrium-of-the-game) approach emphasizes that the central role of both market and nonmarket institutions is to establish a stable structure to human interactions and exchanges by reducing uncertainties arising from incomplete information about behavior of other agents. Thus, if institutions constrain the choices of agents, consistency is difficult to ensure. An important implication of the EG approach to institutional change is that the nonmarket institutions correspond to Nash equilibria, which are multiple in repeated plays, and typically, there are many possible institutional solutions. As Platteau (2008) has shown in the framework of economic growth and development that inefficient institutions may come to be established and sustained over time in poor underdeveloped economies. This follows the existence of multiple equilibria in the Nash equilibrium concept. As Platteau notes:

> Just consider a simple two-agent coordination game in which there are two Nash equilibria in pure strategies, with one equilibrium Pareto dominating the other. For example two measurement systems are available but one is superior to the other, say because it is easier to use. For each agent, to coordinate on the same system is always preferable than to have a mismatch of strategies. Whether the convention established favors the socially efficient or the inefficient system will depend on the content of the shared benefits of the agents and on which equilibrium is a focal point in their minds. The inefficient measurement system may therefore predominate if agents believe that others are going to use it. Moreover once the inefficient convention is established, the very concept of Nash equilibrium that underlies it implies that it may persist for a very long time.

2.5 The Evolutionary View

The evolutionary view (EV) in the institutional approach stresses that rules of institutional change are the outcome of an organic process of Darwinian natural selection, which is similar to the competitive pressures of the market and Adam Smith's concept of "invisible hand." In the orthodox version of the EV model, the institutions such as market and governance that are inefficient are most likely to have a low evolutionary fitness and hence the competitive pressure would replace them in the long run by more efficient institutions.

Three important features of the EV model are to be noted because of their economic implications. First, the process of investing in knowledge capital and the evolution of competitive markets today are characterized by "adaptive learning" as an evolutionary mechanism. Herber Simon (1991) argues that human learning implicit in knowledge innovations works essentially via an adaptive feedback mechanism.

In Darwinian natural selection the central concepts are organisms, populations, fitness, genes, and mutations. In the evolutionary theory of Nelson and Winter (1982) counterparts of these concepts are easily found. Individual firms are organisms, industries are populations, profitability is fitness, routines are genes, and innovations are mutations. Darwinian natural selection entails two mechanisms: a selection mechanism and a replication mechanism. The selection mechanism that Nelson and Winter have in mind seems to be strictly analogous to natural selection. Just as the genes of reproductively successful organisms spread over the gene pool of the population, the profitable routines are spread in the industry at the expense of less profitable ones. An economic evolutionary theory that is based on the selection mechanism needs some replication mechanism to make qualitative predictions about changes in industry behavior. Nelson and Winter treat innovations as the economic equivalent of mutations.

A second aspect of the EV approach emphasized the dynamic changes of the new market structures that have evolved in recent years. The new market structure is sometimes called hypercompetition. This market structure diverges from the neoclassical Walrasian market equilibria in several ways. First of all, it is driven by technology; second it increases various forms of nonprice competition. In recent times these dynamic forces have led to declining prices and costs of the new products and software services resulting in Cournot–Nash type solutions. Following Schumpeter's innovation approach D'Aveni (1994) has characterized this state as hypercompetition. He holds that competitive markets have two facets: static and dynamic. The former takes technology and innovations as given, so firms compete only on prices and costs. But the dynamic force changes technology and innovations at various points of the value chain, thus challenging firms to compete in new innovations, which are "mutants" in biological theory. Thus, the successful firms and industry transform their technology and innovations so as to create new strategic resources and products with increasing profits. New products and marketing technologies tend to create a state of monopoly profits until the other firms catch up. Recently Sengupta and Fanchon (2009) have discussed in some detail this new paradigm of change in modern technology-intensive industries such as computer and telecom industries.

Finally the EV approach uses a more generalized concept of equilibrium, which is fundamentally different from the other approaches. The EV approach believes that the equilibrium concept may be understood only within a dynamic framework. This framework is based on evolutionary game theory, where equilibrium is attained when the properties of different types of agents able to survive have become stable. It follows immediately that the concept of evolutionary efficiency based on the idea of maximizing average fitness differs significantly from the standard economic concepts in either the Pareto or the technological efficiency game. Another illuminating lesson of the EV approach is the path-dependent nature of institutional evolution: small initial differences may entail distinct societal histories to emerge. Because the evolutionary processes follow patterns that have different long-term characteristics depending on their initial starting conditions, the patterns of growth and development are up in different equilibria. Nothing can be said a priori about the comparative levels of efficiency or inefficiency reached by these varied configurations. As North (1990) has emphasized large fixed costs, learning by doing, coordination effects, and adaptive expectations all contribute to creating path dependence. Solow-type models of economic growth seem to ignore these aspects of path dependence caused by all institutional changes, where the market forms a small part of overall growth.

2.6 Market Expansion and Growth

For the last two decades economic growth of national income has been most rapid in the newly developed countries (NICs) of Southeast Asia such as China, Taiwan, South Korea, and Singapore. For example the average GDP growth in China was 10.2% per year during the period 1985–1994. Since then a growth rate of over 9.5% per year has been sustained. The growth experience of other NICs has been very similar. To a large extent this high growth episode has been due to openness in international trade and the fast adoption and development of new technology. In the high-tech fields technology changes the market structure dramatically. Advances in computer and software technology and communication techniques and liberalization of global trade practices have played a most dynamic role in this regard. The emergence of this new economy has helped expand the markets. The internet economy allows the market to expand globally, also intensifying pressure of competition in hypercompetitive markets. Three aspects of this demand explosion are important here. The first is the increase in volume of demand due to globalization of trade. This expansion of trade has firms exploiting economies of scale. Traditional economic theory assumes that over a certain level of production there will be diminishing returns as the scale of production increases. However, as modern economies have undergone a transformation from large-scale material manufacturing to the designing and use of new technologies, the underlying mechanisms shaping economic activity are increasingly characterized by increasing returns. Knowledge intensive products such as computer hardware and software, telecommunications and pharmaceuticals, and the like have all the characteristics subject to increasing returns.

The second aspect of demand growth is due to the significant economies of scale in demand rather than supply. Since the value of a network goes up as the square of the number of users, demand growth has generated further investment in expanding the networks through interlocking and other linkages. Finally the globalization of trade and demand and the use of information technology (IT) networks in communication and other high-tech industries imply that US growth of IT technology will have a diffusion and spillover effect on other countries of Asia and Latin America and Europe.

In the high-tech industries of today, investments in knowledge capital have played a crucial role as engines of growth. Many of the subsectors of the IT and communication sectors specializing in software services and managerial skills in the arena of international "outsourcing" are highly labor-intensive. They export the spillover benefits of global R&D and innovation technology. Modern models of endogenous growth theory have attempted to incorporate these spillover effects and the impact of market expansion in sustaining economic growth rates in the long run. The growth experiences of NICs in Asia have provided support to this worldview of expanding export markets.

Chapter 3
Investment

Traditionally, investment is viewed as additions to the stock of physical capital. In the classical school Adam Smith emphasized the role of physical capital and technological progress as basic to expanding economic growth. The specialization for labor and free trade provided the source of economic efficiency of capitalist development. The classical school employed the concept of an aggregate production function, where aggregate output depends on labor (L), physical capital (K), and technology (T). The production function is assumed to be subject to diminishing returns to each input. The growth of the labor force is presumed in the short run to be proportional to the rate of capital accumulation, i.e., the more rapid the pace of capital accumulation, the faster the rate of overall economic growth. The rate of physical capital accumulation, which equals gross investment, is determined by the rate of profit earned by the capitalist investors. In the post-Keynesian theory Harrod and Domar used this capital accumulation argument as central to economic growth.

They assumed a linear production function, which implies constant returns to scale. They introduced the concept of the *warranted rate of growth*, which is the rate of growth of total output consistent with equilibrium in both input and output markets. This output growth rate ($\Delta Y/Y$) equals the ration s/v, where s is the savings rate and v is the constant capital–output ratio. If total output Y also grows over time at the same rate s/v, then the economy will be in steady-state equilibrium, such that Y, K, and K/L all grow at the same rate. Thus, an increase in the savings rate, which allows a higher level of investment and capital goods creation, will increase the growth rate of the economy, ceteris paribus. Technology is assumed to be given in the model. Three aspects of the Harrod–Domar model are most important. One is that the equilibrium growth rate in the model is found to be quite unstable, i.e., it is sometimes called knife-edge stability. For if output (Y) grows at a rate faster (slower) than the warranted rate (s/v), then the investors would react by investing and producing even more (even less) output in the next period. This type of instability is due to the assumption of fixed labor and capital coefficients in the production function, i.e., $L=b\ Y$ and $K=v\ Y$ with b and v as positive constants. The second feature of the model is that physical capital is the most dominant input. Demand for capital or investment is the key to generate employment.

J. Sengupta, *Understanding Economic Growth: Modern Theory and Experience*,
DOI 10.1007/978-1-4419-8026-7_3,

Hence, in periods of economic depression when unemployment is high, any public policy for increasing investment would provide stimulus for employment and growth. It is thus an extension of the short-run Keynesian model. Third, technology is assumed to be exogenous in the model, so any dynamic shift of the production function is not considered.

Two policy implications of the Harrod–Domar model are important. One is that this model has influenced the state planning of development in less-developed countries during 1980s and 1990s greatly. Emphasis on the key variables of economic development such as the rate of saving, the level of overall physical capital investment in the private sector, the need for investment in the public sector, and the capital intensity measured by the capital–output ratio was central to public policy decisions. Most often, this led to the formulation and implementation and successive 5-year plans. Second, the state support to augment the investment rate in the developing countries such as India often resulted in large public investment in the capital-intensive industries such as machinery, chemicals, and machine tools. Indirectly this strategy transformed the technological composition of GDP. This meant that technology did undergo some change through a dynamic shift of the overall capital–output ratio.

3.1 Solow's Growth Model

Solow's growth model adopted the standard neoclassical assumption that labor and capital inputs are infinitely substitutable in production, though such substitution is subject to diminishing returns. Instead of assuming that the production isoquants for firms and industries formed right angles, implying no substitution of inputs as in the Harrod–Domar model, Solow assumed the production isoquants to be smoothly convex to the origin. This removed the knife-edge instability of the Harrod–Domar model. Thus, for any rate of saving, the Solow model predicted a steady-state equilibrium level of income per capita and the instability of the Harrod–Domar model disappeared.

The investment model of Solow (1956, 1957) has four basic features for economic growth. First, the Solow model assumed a standard neoclassical production function with decreasing returns to capital and then taking the rates of saving and population growth as exogenous it showed that these two variables determine the steady-state level of income per capita. Because saving and population growth vary across countries, different countries reach different steady states. The steady-state equation shows that the higher the rate of saving or investment, the richer the country and that the higher the rate of population growth, the poorer the country. Note that per capita income is used as a measure of richer or poorer level of living. Second, the technology (T) in the production function $Y=F(L, K, T)$ is assumed to be exogenous, not affected by the market conditions, but the two factors labor and capital are used at an optimal level by the conditions of a perfectly competitive market so that factors are paid their marginal products. The final growth equation for steady-state per capita income derived in the model shows that it grows over time at the percentage rate g, where g is the exponential growth rate of technology i.e., $\Delta y/y(t)=g$, $g>0$ where $y=Y/L$ is the per capita income. Third, the Solow model makes an important distinction between the level effect and the growth effect when per capita income rises. Two variables, savings rate and population, affect the *level* of long-run income per capita $y(t)$, but not its growth measured by the percentage growth $\Delta y/y(t)$ of per capita income. Thus, technology measured by the shift of production frontier, which is also called total factor productivity (TFP), has a *growth effect* over time since it induces growth in long run income per capita. The effects of technological progress are captured in the Solow model by the proxy variable represented by long-run time trend, which reflects the influence of omitted variables other than physical capital and labor. Finally, Solow (1957) applied the model to the time series data for the US economy and found the surprising result that the US output growth in the first half of the twentieth century could be mostly attributed to technological progress measured by the TFP growth g. For example the annual TFP growth was estimated to be 2.25% during 1930–1949 and 1.5% during 1909–1949. This line of research stimulated the upsurge of many growth-accounting exercises that are summarized in Mankiew, Romer, and Weil (1992).

Two major extensions of the Solow model have been made in recent times. One is by Mankiew et al. (1992) who included human capital along with physical capital and constructed an augmented Solow model, where the enrollment in secondary-level education is used as a proxy for human capital. They showed that the accumulation of physical capital has a higher impact on income per capita than the original Solow model. A higher saving rate leads to higher income in steady state, which in turn leads to a higher level of human capital, even if the rate of human capital accumulation is unchanged. Higher saving thus raises total factor productivity (TFP) as it is usually measured. A second modification of the Solow model came from the historical evidence in favor of viewing industrial innovation and technology driven by profits and the incentive to exploit new markets. Thus, technology is more endogenous and market driven. As the modern models of endogenous growth imply, technological improvements typically raise productivity of both physical and knowledge (skill) capital and thereby induce additional investments. This aspect was ignored in the original Solow model.

3.2 Endogenous Growth

Recent growth models are called endogenous because they challenge the basic assumption of the Solow model that technology alone determines the long-run growth of income per capita and that this technology is assumed to be completely exogenous in the sense that it is unaffected by profits and market incentives. In the late 1980s the endogenous growth theory emerged. This theory did not find physical capital accumulation to be the dominant factor in spurring economic growth. Also, it introduced some important inputs such as knowledge capital and learning by doing, which do not obey diminishing returns. This means that a country's short-run production function could generate increasing returns and hence permanent increases in income per capita. Also endogenous growth theory presumes that technological change is endogenous to the economy and determined by market forces. In endogenous growth models a higher level of investment, which includes both physical and human capital, not only increases per capita income but can also sustain high and even rising rates of income growth over the future. This is simply not possible within the neoclassical Solow-type growth model, where once the steady-state equilibrium level of income is reached, it remains unchanged unless the exogenous technology shifts the production function upward.

One simple form of endogenous growth model is the AK model:

$$Y(t) = A(k)K(t)$$

with income (Y) a linear function of $K(t)$, which is redefined as a measure of the combined stock of human, physical, and knowledge (e.g., research) capital. Here $A = A(k)$ denotes the induced or endogenous technological change. Different economies will have distinct $A(k)$ values, depending on the feedback mechanisms affecting knowledge creation, adaptation, and the diffusion of technological change. The speed of any country's technological progress is conditional of the following:

(a) The education level of the labor force and types of investment in R&D
(b) Learning by adapting or improving better technology from abroad through foreign direct investment or technology imports
(c) The economy's institutional and organizational capabilities in the form of flexibility, transparency, and productive efficiency

One basic premise of the endogenous growth theory is that technology or knowledge is in part a private good determined by the market forces of profit and loss, e.g., the products of pharmaceuticals or software development. Technology is not the A of the Solow model, available equally and identically to all countries exogenously as if it were a costless public good.

Endogenous growth models suggest that government policies can definitely affect the rate of long-term economic growth by impacting the accumulation of both physical and human capital and the effort devoted to R&D and the creation and diffusion of new knowledge through software development and other services provided by the new information technology.

The AK model assumes nondiminishing returns but differs from the Harrod–Domar model in two respects. One is that its input K combines both physical and knowledge (human) capital, and the variable $A = A(k)$ embodies endogenous technology. Both Lucas (1993) and Romer (1990) considered a Cobb–Douglas production function with increasing returns to scale. This is more general than the constant returns assumption of the AK model. Endogeneity in the Lucas and Romer model is from intentional investment decisions made by entrepreneurs seeking to maximize profits and earn quasi-monopoly rents due to "first mover" advantages. Thus, new technology in the form of composite human capital accumulation is not a public good but a nontrivial input complementary to all other inputs. This knowledge capital (i.e., a form of human capital) is a nonrival input and hence helps all other inputs in a complementary way. This input is only partially excludable, since the form of R&D (e.g., software development) yields spillover or external benefits. Due to nonconvexity introduced by the non-rival input the aggregate production function exhibits increasing returns to scale. This implies that the growth effect in the Solow sense can be generated by the non-rival inputs in the form of knowledge capital. Clearly competitive equilibrium cannot be supported here. Instead one has to seek Cournot–Nash equilibria in the framework of monopolistic competition. In this framework Lucas introduced several new dimensions of endogenous technology. He pointed out that Asian growth miracles (e.g., high and sustained economic growth rates over 1965–2000 in the five Asian countries: Japan, Hong Kong, South Korea, Singapore, and Taiwan) cannot be simply explained by physical capital accumulation alone. One has to introduce the dynamic role of human capital accumulation in schools, colleges, and research institutions and the training and skill development on the job. The rate of expansion of knowledge and skills in both forms, on the job and at schools and colleges transforms a *level effect* into a *growth effect* in the language of the Solow model. This notion of knowledge capital is important for its "learning-by-doing effect," a term coined by Arrow (1962) to capture the cumulative productivity increase in the aircraft industry. Learning has two types of impact. One is that it increases the total stock of design knowledge by increasing its efficiency. The second is that knowledge capital employed in research and job training leads to an expansion of the stock of design knowledge. As a result the unit cost of producing new designs declines over time, e.g., development of new software.

Lucas has stressed the concept of learning spillover technology as an important feature of endogenous technology. This spillover is the source of rapid productivity growth due to increasing returns to scale. To the question why does not capital flow from rich to poor countries on a large scale, the answer provided by the Lucas model is that the spillover effect is very small in poor countries. Another dimension of spillover technology is that for such learning to continue on a long-run sustained basis, the labor, management, and entrepreneurs must work continually to improve the technology through what Grossman and Helpman (1991) called "the quality ladder," i.e., improvement of quality over time.

The central premise of the modern endogenous growth theory is the emphasis placed on the effectiveness with which a country's endowments, e.g., human and physical capital, other resources, and knowledge capital, are utilized in the production process. And in today's world with such rapidly expanding knowledge and technology creation and diffusion, the countries must follow the path of efficiency in technical change. The production frontier must improve over time by shifting to the right. Also, the dynamics of comparative advantage in international trade dictates that a fast-growing country captures the dynamic gains from the expanding world trade by reducing its exports costs on a comparative basis. The experience of rapid growth in Southeast Asia bears ample testimony to this efficiency-improving episode.

3.3 Foreign Direct Investment

Foreign direct investment (FDI) implies the ownership of productive assets by a parent corporation in another nation. The World Investment Report 2006 by UNCTAD estimated that the developing nations had accumulated a stock of $2.8 trillion of FDI: $1.55 trillion in East and South Asia, $937 billion in Latin America, and $151 billion in Africa. Overall, the stock of FDI has grown at an impressive rate. In 1990 the ratio of FDI stock to world GDP was 8.5, increasing to 22.7 by 2005. This increasing trend has continued as of 2010.

Some important characteristics of FDI in global trade have to be noted. First, one has to distinguish between the *stock* and flow of FDI. The flow of FDI is the annual change in the stock. While nearly 28% of total stock of FDI of the developed nations was invested in the less-developed world, the flow has increasingly been directed to the less developed world. During the period 2003–2006 an estimated 34% of these FDI flows went to the developing nations as reported by UNCTAD. The ratio of FDI flows to GDP has increased from 0.79% in 1975 to 2.34% in 2000 for a broad sample of 59 representative developing nations. This trend has continued as of 2010. Second, multinational corporations (MNCs) operate in two or more nations with a significant equity investment of 10% or more in a foreign branch plant of subsidiary. By 1992 US MNCs owned 25.3% of all of the direct FDI spread around the globe. But the investment activity abroad by MNCs took a dramatic turn in the late 1980s, mainly due to the revolutions in information technology in communication, transportation, and megamergers. Here the motivation for investment was not the domestic market, but the expanding world market. New manufacturing activities spread in the less-developed economies based upon their cheap labor and flexible legal system with less environmental restrictions. Skilled man power in certain areas such as information technology and software services also helped to lower unit costs of production and distribution. The phenomenal growth in total output and exports in the Southeast-Asian countries such as Singapore, South Korea, Hong Kong, China, and Taiwan bear ample testimony to the emergence of globally integrated production system, where the MNCs evolved with advances in technology, from the cellular communications to the computer and data-entry services. Since the 1990s the global production and distribution networks are typically centered on a series of strategic alliances and implicit collaborations among the MNCs, which sometimes include the entrepreneurial groups from the Third-World countries and also NICs from Asia. Manufacturing exports from these countries back to the world markets are central to the new paradigm, while the export flows from the advanced countries to the developing economies increasingly take the form of services, intangibles, and R&D investments. Outsourcing of jobs and services from the developed countries and export processing zones in the developing countries such as India, China, Taiwan, and South Korea helped these countries to reap the benefits of export trade and also capture the external gains from the spillover technology developed in the West.

The US-based MNCs continued to dominate the global production patterns till 1960, but it declined in recent years. In 1960 the US MNCs accounted for 49% of the total stock of FDI, but by 1992 the share shrank to just 25%, falling to 19% in 2005.

The European Union in 2005 held 51.3% of the total accumulated stock of FDI, up from 45.2% in 2000. This increasing diversity of FDI sources tends to strengthen the relative bargaining power of the developing nations such as China and India. Thus, FDI and MNC activities in developing countries have contributed significantly to the investment climate of these countries. For example during the period 2003–2005 the average level of FDI expressed as a percentage of new capital formation was 10.9%. It has increased since then in recent times. The share of world exports from developing nations in the high-skill technology-intensive manufactures has increased from 20.2% in 1980 to about 32%.

There are some economic pitfalls from the FDI investment and MNC activities in the developing countries. One is that it sets up some barriers to the growth of domestic indigenous technology. It may also stifle the R&D investment for the domestic entrepreneurs. For countries such as India, it has led the domestic entrepreneurs to adopt the easy way of a managing agency system, where the Indian companies only provide services instead of developing or using new technology. This is in striking contrast to the pattern in Japan and Taiwan, where they borrow the foreign technology and improve on it and then export their own technology-intensive products. One notes that India does not figure in the list of 25 core innovating countries as measured by the average annual US patents granted per million population. Japan ranks second (273 patents), Taiwan third (241 patents), Singapore ninth (97 patents), South Korea fourteenth (79.8) patents, and India is somewhere in 50th position with only one patent.

A second impact of FDI is the unambiguous positive partial correlation between the FDI stock and the inequality of income distribution measured by the Gini coefficient. This had been confirmed by the empirical studies by several economists. The so-called Kuznets hypothesis also asserts a similar result. This implies the need for remedial state policies in two directions. One is the need for an appropriate tax and fiscal policy and the second is the need for a dispersal and decentralization of new technology. Taiwan provides a unique example of the second aspect. Its rapid rise in R&D investment was concentrated on firms with fewer than 100 employees. As a result the technology diffusion helped improve the middle class. Also the government in Taiwan encouraged the creation of venture capital funds to provide capital for the new start-up enterprises, which actively participated in the process of technology transfer and diffusion. As a result it did not increase the Gini coefficient. The only country that offers an exception to the Kuznets hypothesis is Taiwan, where growth occurred along with the benefits of development and technological progress. There is a clear need for other developing countries to follow Taiwan's model of growth with equity.

3.4 Investment and Increasing Returns

Adam Smith stressed that the key to industry growth and economic development is division of labor and specialization, which reduce the unit cost of production and increase efficiency of the competitive system. The market sets up the limit for this cost-reducing process. Recently the globalization of trade in technology-intensive products and software development has dramatically widened the size of the market. The so-called "four tigers" of Southeast Asia, Singapore, South Korea, Hong Kong (China), and Taiwan, have dramatically exploited this growth in market size to compete very successfully in augmenting its exports and overall national growth rate. Two important impacts of this growth in market size are as follows. One is that the NICs have undergone a structural transformation from large-scale material manufacturing to the design and use of new technologies and that this dramatic change is increasingly characterized by increasing returns (IR). These technologies generate mechanisms of positive feedback that act to reinforce successful economic efficiency. They occur due to four basic reasons: (1) high fixed costs and very low variable costs, (2) network economies, i.e., the value of a product or service, e.g., windows in computers, increases with the number of users, (3) high switching costs so that customers stay with the product for some time, and (4) scale economies to firms due to growth in industry-level knowledge capital. The second impact of globalization is in changing the market structure of world trade and in challenging the guiding principles of the competitive equilibria. In this new world of innovations and spillover of R&D effects, various forms of noncompetitive market structures have evolved in recent times through mergers and acquisitions and also collaborations in R&D and other network links. The forward and backward linkage effects of this new technology have cumulative effects. Investment in knowledge capital affects both demand and supply sides. On the demand side the spillover effect spreads through network externalities. On the supply side (i.e., backward linkage) it spurs other industries to improve the existing software and thereby innovate.

International business theory suggests that MNCs possess certain firm-specific advantages, allowing them to overcome the disadvantages of foreignness and compete successfully against local firms. These advantages deal with the following: (1) innovative capabilities, (2) scale economies, (3) competitive advantage through differentiation, (4) flexibility of organizational structure, and (5) networking.

The knowledge embodied in new products, new services, and proprietary technology is widely regarded as premier advantages for the MNCs. Owing to certain characteristics of the IR process, the potential advantages from the commercial exploitation of new knowledge are likely to be considerable, exceeding those of the traditional DR (diminishing returns) industries. Using panel data for 190 IR industries over the period 1989–1998 for FDI from the USA, Nachum (2002) estimated, by regression methods, the role of innovative capabilities measured by R&D expenditure as percentage of sales. His result confirms the strong explanatory power of innovative capabilities. Also, the explanatory power of scale economies, flexibility and networking in explaining the FDI intensity, was found to be strong and statistically significant. Scale economies have traditionally been regarded as a major firm-specific advantage of MNCs. Large firms have been perceived as being endowed with the tangible and intangible assets conducive to foreign activity and the ability to acquire and learn new technology and know-how. Nachum's regression estimates used size measured in terms of sales of affiliates and number of patents and focused its impact on FDI.

These specific advantages of IR processes are useful in two ways for the developing countries. One is that the domestic entrepreneurs have to adopt similar strategies to compete with MNCs. The second is that the state should adopt policy measures so that these advantages and learning capabilities are shared with the domestic industries. Clearly Japan and the successful NICs in Southeast Asia have adopted these strategies. For example Japan has challenged the US for international industrial leadership since the 1950s. In 1950 Japan's per capita GDP was only 20% of that of the USA, whereas in 1992 it rose to 90%. The industries where the challenge came include high-tech fields such as automobiles, electronics, and machine tools. The fast growing NICs in Asia such as Taiwan, South Korea, and China have successfully competed in most areas of information technology such as software, semiconductors, and electronic equipment. Organizational learning and improving the borrowed technology have played key roles for the success of NICs achieving significant competitive advantages.

Globalization has changed the world market structure most drastically in recent times. Competitive pressure has increased, and the presence of significant IR in new industries disrupted the guiding principles of competitive equilibria. The new market structure that has evolved in these new industries such as computers, telecommunications, and pharmaceuticals is dominated by large firms that enjoy increasing returns through investment in R&D and knowledge capital. This market structure has been called by D'Aveni (1994) as hypercompetition. A hypercompetitive market structure diverges from a competitive market structure in several ways. First of all, it is driven by knowledge capital and various investments in dynamic innovations. Second, it augments the various forms of nonprice competition. Mergers and acquisitions, cooperative alliances in R&D networks, and significant investment in long-run knowledge capital have led to declining prices and unit costs resulting in Cournot–Nash type solutions. The hypercompetition emphasized the dynamic competition as opposed to the static competition. The static competition takes knowledge capital and information technology as given so that firms compete only on prices and costs. Dynamic competition shifts the production frontier upward so that firms compete in new innovations. Three new areas of cost efficiency are central to hypercompetition: innovation efficiency, access efficiency, and resource efficiency. These are the core of dynamic efficiency, which is much different from the concepts of production and allocative efficiency underlying static competition. This dynamic efficiency can be better understood if we view efficiency as an escalation ladder, where the firms compete by racing up the ladder. Thus, racing up the escalation ladder in the arena of R&D investment, know-how for new processes and products, and new software development constitutes innovation efficiency. Access efficiency involves racing up the ladder in the strongholds arena. By building barriers around a stronghold, the firms reap quasi-monopoly profits in protected markets (e.g., patenting sometimes is used). Porter (1980) identifies six major barriers to entry that the firms use to create and sustain a stronghold, e.g., dynamic economies of scale due to a shift in the production frontier, product differentiation, large capital requirements, high switching costs, access to specific channels of distribution and specific advantages such as access to low-cost sources of raw materials and skilled manpower. Finally the dynamic resourcefulness of firms involving the creation of new strategic assets at various points in the chain generates resource efficiency. This has been called the area of "deep pockets" by D'Aveni. Companies seek to find the best use for their resources or assets by going over a global setting. This is sometimes facilitated by the role of MNCs. Hypercompetitive firms must use their assets to build their next temporary advantage before their competition. For example IBM bet the company on the 360 series computers, and the bet paid off during the 1960s. But it could not sustain the position because it failed to keep up a strong position in the next phase of temporary advantage, e.g., the PC market. Instead tiny companies such as Apple and Microsoft became giants by seizing the next advantage. Apple and its iPod and iPad products provide a significant example of successful racing along the escalation ladder of resource efficiency. This rivalry between firms in hypercompetition creates a pressure to improve and innovate new assets and resources and to lower costs over time.

Thus, we conclude that competition to improve economic efficiency provides the pressure for firms to invest in R&D and other forms of innovations. As a result the market structure becomes highly hypercompetitive. Dynamic models of differential games are often used in the current literature to characterize the equilibrium paths. Sengupta and Fanchon (2009) have discussed in some detail these dynamic models, which challenge the guiding principles of Walrasian competitive equilibria. These models of market games are intended to explain the two economic processes at work. One is the set of strategies by firms intended to affect the current conduct of rivals and the other by altering the market structures in such ways that constrain the rival's subsequent future strategies.

Chapter 4
Innovation

Innovation is a broader concept than technology. It includes both technology and knowledge capital. Technology is based mainly on the accumulation of physical capital. Knowledge capital and know-how are based on the accumulation of human capital. Human capital may take several forms, e.g., R&D investment, learning by doing, organizational learning, and creative forms of research applications. Schumpeter's concept of innovation is very broad: it plays a central role in speeding up capitalist development. It fundamentally alters the paradigm of Walrasian competitive equilibrium: it shifts the production frontier, develops new products and processes, and changes the market structure. To quote Schumpeter (1947, p. 84):

> As soon as quality competition and sales effort are admitted into sacred precincts of theory, the price variable is ousted from its dominant position... But in capitalist reality as distinguished from its textbook picture it is not that kind of competition which counts but the competition from the new country, the new technology- competition which commands a decisive cost or quality advantage and which strikes not at the margins of projects and the outputs of the existing firms but at their foundations and their very lives. This kind of competition is as much more effective than the other as a bombardment is in comparison with forcing a door.

Schumpeter considered dynamic efficiency creation by large firms as central to innovation, and he emphasized "the process of creative destruction" and "diffusion" as twin processes associated with innovation. By creative destruction firms discard old technology in favor of new ones. They shift to higher production frontiers. And by creative diffusion the firms help to spread the creative knowledge and skill across the network through alliances and cooperative ventures in R&D and basic research. In the modern terminology of endogenous growth theory, most of creative diffusion occurs through the spillover effects of innovation and externalities of R&D investment at the industry level. Both Romer and Lucas have emphasized this; externalities play a dynamic role by which one innovation leads to another and by which the diffusion process becomes endemic.

J. Sengupta, *Understanding Economic Growth: Modern Theory and Experience*,
DOI 10.1007/978-1-4419-8026-7_4, © Springer Science+Business Media, LLC 2011

4.1 Growth Miracles

Baumol (2002) discussed five most important preconditions to explain the unprecedented and unparalleled growth performance of the developed capitalist economies. The record of high and sustained economic growth in Asia in the last three decades enjoyed by countries such as Japan, the four "tigers" (Hong Kong, South Korea, Singapore, and Taiwan), and Indonesia, Malaysia, and Thailand has been characterized as a growth miracle by Lucas (1993) and other modern economists. Recently, China and India have joined the list of high-performing Asian economies, and Sengupta (2005, 2010) has recently analyzed the sources of innovation efficiency in these countries.

Five explanatory influences for the growth miracle of free enterprise discussed by Baumol include the following:

1. Oligopolistic competition among large high-tech business firms with innovation as the prime competitive weapon.
2. Routinization of innovative activities and thereby minimizing the uncertainty of the innovative process. It is estimated that some 70% of US R&D investment is now done by private industry, much of it incorporated into firms' day-to-day activities.
3. Productive entrepreneurship encouraged by entrepreneurs to devote themselves to productive innovation rather than unproductive pursuit of short-term economic profits such as setting barriers to market entry.
4. The rule of law, which includes strategies for immunity of property from arbitrary expropriation.
5. Technology selling and trading to secure opportunities for profitable dissemination of innovations.

Oligopolistic competition is the most important explanatory influence in the above list because of two reasons. One is that it yields a game theoretic equilibrium, which challenges the Walrasian principles of competitive equilibrium. The other reason is that innovation has replaced price as the name of the game in a number of important industries such as computers, telecommunications, and pharmaceuticals.

In his analysis of growth miracles in the fast-growing Southeast Asian countries, Lucas emphasized two aspects of innovations. One is the spillover effect and the other the complementary nature of the innovation input in the form of knowledge capital. Most innovations have significant spillover effects, which mean that a considerable share of the benefits of a particular innovation goes without compensation to the original innovators, but to firms who have made no contribution to the discovery and development of that particular innovation. Thus, the fast-growing NICs of Southeast Asia including China and India in recent years have taken advantage of new innovations developed in the Western developed countries but spilled over in the NICs in Asia. Japan did very well to adopt, imitate, and improve the advanced technology of the West. Recent spread and diffusion of information technology have intensified this process. A major adverse impact of spillover is that it discourages the original innovators to invest optimal amounts for innovations. This private investment for innovation falls below the socially optimal level. But Spence (1984) and others have shown that appropriate public tax–subsidy policy can be easily devised to correct this gap between the private and social optima.

The complementary nature of innovation emphasizes the nonrivalrous nature of the innovation input in the form of R&D and human capital. It helps all other inputs grow in productivity. Thus, one innovation provides incentives and opportunities for other innovations, and the growth of productivity of other inputs helps expand the market by lowering unit costs and prices. Also learning by doing helps the cumulative impact of innovation particularly in the high-tech information-based industries, such as computers, communications, and pharmaceuticals.

Sengupta has discussed in some detail the process of technology diffusion and learning by doing in China and Taiwan. The Taiwan model stimulated the diffusion process through subcontracting IT jobs to SMEs (small manufacturing enterprises). China favored town and village enterprises (TVEs); hence, fiscal incentives and direct government subsidies are needed in the initial stage. India needs to adopt such a policy in its IT sector. The successful NICs in Asia achieved innovation efficiency and its diffusion through five broad economic policies:

1. Human capital deepening
2. Creation of publicly financed research centers
3. Fiscal incentives for private R&D investments
4. Economic incentives for information technology like computer industry and electronics
5. Technology transfer through FDI in information technology-intensive sectors and industries

Sengupta (2005) has reviewed the comparative performance of India in the context of NICs in Asia, using data on an R&D index comprising several components such as high-technology exports as a proportion of total manufacturing export, the number of engineers and scientists in R&D as a percentage of GDP, and the average annual number of industrial patents. Selected ranking are as follows: Japan (1), USA (3), Singapore (6), South Korea (13), Malaysia (16), China (20), and Indonesia (22). Although this index is very rough, it shows one thing very clearly, i.e., how far China and India have to improve on the R&D and innovation front.

4.2 Innovation Models

Dynamic models of innovation efficiency characterize the long-run process of economic growth through a number of factors. We discuss here four important models and their characterization of the innovation dynamics.

1. A dynamic model of industry evolution through R&D investment by Folster and Trofimov (1997)
2. A model of survival of the fittest through growth efficiency by Sengupta (2003)
3. Schumpeterian model of creative destruction and diffusion of innovation
4. A feedback model by Baumol (2002), where an increase in R&D expenditure stimulates productivity growth with a time lag and productivity growth causes a change in price. Price change stimulates the R&D demand and the output level of R&D activity

The industry evolution model has two sources of industry growth. One is the knowledge spillover from one firm to others. This knowledge spread often finds new applications or stimulates further innovation activity in other firms. When these externalities are sufficiently strong, an industry can exhibit aggregate IR to scale. The scale economies offer a potent force of industry growth. The other source of industry growth is the quality improvement due to R&D investment and corresponding decline in quality-adjusted prices, which stimulates overall demand and expands the market. As a result the leaders in the Bertrand price game earn higher expected quasi-monopoly profits, which may stimulate further innovation. This model shows that R&D externalities can imply ranges of aggregate increasing returns to scale in R&D investment. As a consequence several equilibria can exist with different numbers of firms and different R&D investment levels in industry. Their empirical application over Swedish industrial firms during 1988–1990 supports the notion of multiple equilibria and an S-shaped profit curve. This profit curve implies that profits tend to decrease initially as the number of competitors increases, but there exists other ranges where R&D externalities imply increased profits as the number of firms increases. An interesting hypothesis of this model deals with market entry or increasing market share for the successful firms who lead by reducing unit costs and prices and improving quality. This incentive of higher expected profits provides the source of new innovations and large R&D investment. For computers, semiconductors, and pharmaceuticals this trend has been consistently adopted by the successful high-tech industries.

Two comments are in order. First, the model challenges the paradigm of the Walrasian competitive equilibria and shows that multiple equilibria in Cournot–Bertrand game theory framework may involve cyclical movements in the industry performance. Some equilibria are stable; the race in the quality ladder between the oligopolistic firms is motivated largely by the incentive of high expected profits so that innovation is endogenous and incentive-driven.

The dynamic efficiency model by Sengupta (2003, 2007) emphasizes the premise that technology as innovations affects the market structure significantly. Competition has two facets: static and dynamic. The former takes technology as given, so firms compete only on costs and prices. Thus, greater competition reduces prices and raises unit costs, thereby reducing profits. In the limit some firms may have to exit. Dynamic competition, however, changes technology at various points of the value chain, thus challenging firms to compete in new ways. In this framework, growth efficiency (i.e., growth of output) rather than level efficiency (i.e., level of output) is a better frontier. Successful firms attain growth efficiency and sustain R&D efforts to remain on the growth efficiency frontier. At the industry level this intensifies the exit rate for declining market share of firms, which fails to maintain the leading edge of the dynamic production and cost frontier. This provides support to the principle of survival of the fittest, as the successful firms apply innovation efficiency to increase their dominance and leadership position. D'Aveni (1994) has characterized this oligopolistic structure as hypercompetition. Three key areas of efficiency central to hypercompetition are innovation efficiency, access efficiency, and resource efficiency. These forms of dynamic efficiency are quite different from the production and allocation efficiency of firms analyzed in Walrasian competitive equilibrium. We may view dynamic efficiency as an escalation ladder. Thus, innovation efficiency involves racing up the ladder in the area of R&D investment for new products, processes, software, and knowledge. This creates new knowledge and know-how, which undermine the positions of incumbent competition. Access efficiency is different from innovation efficiency. It involves racing up the escalation ladder in the stronghold area. By building barriers around a stronghold (e.g., new product or process), the successful firms can reap monopoly profits in a protected market that can be used to fund aggressive price strategies or other innovation investments. Porter (1990) has identified six major barriers to entry that the firms use to create and sustain a stronghold, e.g., dynamic economies of scale, product differentiation, large capital requirements for entering firms, large switching costs, access to favorable distribution channels and favorable locations.

Dynamic resourcefulness of firms involving the creation of new strategic assets at various points of the value chain generates resource efficiency. This has been called "the deep pockets area" by D'Aveni (1994). Companies seek to find the best use for their resources or assets even going over to a global setting. Hypercompetitive firms must use their assets to build their next temporary advantage before their competition. For example, IBM bet on the 360 series computers, and the bet paid off in the 1960s. But it could not sustain the position because it failed to keep up a strong position in the next temporary advantage, e.g., the PC market. Instead tiny firms such as Apple and Microsoft became giants by seizing the market.

The Schumpeterian model of innovation emphasizes two processes. One is the process of creative destruction, and the other is that of creative diffusion. Both processes have the twin objectives of reducing costs and increasing the opportunity for monopoly or quasi-monopoly profits. Hence, Schumpeterian innovation is entirely endogenous. Market selection process determines the survival of firms in an industry and their growth or decline. Schumpeterian dynamics emphasizes the innovation process in the selection process. This innovation produces both substitution-cum-diffusion and evolution, and these effects are generally nonlinear over time, resulting in multiple equilibria, some of which are stable and some unstable. Frequently this innovation stream has been viewed as a stochastic process evolving over time like an epidemic with contagion effects. Assuming the set of innovations to be discrete and large, it may be represented by a set of integers $N(1)$, $N(2),\ldots N(m)$, where $N(i)$ may denote the number of production units or plants or software using that technology. The transition of plants from one innovation technology to another may then be viewed as a birth and death stochastic process, i.e., a Markov process where birth may involve new plants or new software entering the system and death may indicate the exit rate of old plants closing down. Also the set of integers may represent quality ladders, where the latter plants indicate higher quality. The birth and death process model may be viewed in several forms, namely, genetic evolution theory, diffusion of innovations across other firms and other industries, and finally the market selection process, where the new entrants introduce new technology and innovations to displace the incumbent. Sengupta (2004) has discussed in some detail these three forms of innovation dynamics.

Two important implications of the birth and death process model of Schumpeterian dynamics have to be mentioned here. One is the creation of learning-by-doing scale economies by which the new innovating firm gains a cost advantage. If the cost advantage is significantly large, its possessor may elect to set prices so low as to deter the entry by other competitors. Thus, the successful innovating firms may have profit incentive to lead by introducing new products or services. The other implication is that the production capacity of the new innovating firms must be optimally built up for the new innovation technology to displace the old. Aghion and Howitt (1992) have developed a model of creative destruction in Schumpeterian dynamics, which postulates that a successful innovator drives out the previous incumbent by undercutting his process and creating a local monopoly through either a patent or a stronghold, until driven out by the next successful innovator.

When the birth rate exceeds the death rate, the industry grows. This growth is then diffused as others tend to imitate and adopt learning-by-doing methods. Stochastic models of diffusion can capture this spread and spillover effects. These models are intended to capture the contagion and infection effects by which innovation, e.g., a new software, by one firm infects other firms by the lure of high monopoly profits.

Finally we discuss the feedback model of R&D investments by Baumol (2002). This model assumes two sources of R&D output. One is price sensitive, and the other is insensitive. It is based on three premises. The first premise is that R&D investment causes the rate of growth of productivity $g(t)$ outside R&D industries in period t. The second premise is that R&D output $y(t)$ grows proportionally to the growth in productivity. Third, there exists an R&D demand function, which assumes that the demand growth is proportional to the percentage decline in prices. Assuming demand equals supply; the three premises jointly imply a logistic time path of R&D output with two equilibrium levels. Two implicit assumptions of this model are that the productivity growth reduces unit costs and total output for the innovating firms and that this causes competitive price declines, which help stimulate overall demand.

The logistic time path of R&D output has one equilibrium steady state as the upper asymptote. The active role played in this time path is by the price-sensitive R&D

activity. The role of price-insensitive R&D is exogenous. It may induce the firm to undertake a substantial increase in the resources allocated to innovation.

The reason why the upper asymptotic level of steady state is reached in the Baumol model is as follows: As information produced by R&D becomes relatively more costly, other inputs tend to be substituted for information in the production process. For example when R&D costs rise, a firm wanting to increase its output may decide not to invest more in R&D, but instead to buy additional machines of the existing type. Thus, the rising cost of the innovation process can reduce the derived demand for innovator activity. This in turn impedes productivity growth, thus reversing the uptrend in output growth.

This model differs from the Lucas model, where the innovation input like R&D exhibits increasing returns to scale and also complementary effects on other inputs. The Baumol model stresses, however, several characteristics of the feedback of innovation as a self-nourishing process as follows.

1. Innovation in one arena induces further innovations in the same and other arenas.
2. Competition stimulates innovation, and innovation stimulates oligopolistic competition.
3. Foreign trade and open market competition stimulate each other, thereby stimulating innovation. The growth experience of successful NICs in Asia provides ample examples of this stimulating process.
4. Innovation extends the supply of limited resources. For example improving efficiency standards in automobiles helps the conservation of oil resources for future use. This innovation generates impetus for growth-favorable policies in the private and public sectors.
5. Innovation has an acceleration effect on production, i.e., the rate of growth of GDP is an increasing function of the level of innovation. This acceleration relationship applies innovation generally, so that if the market leads firms to allocate a constant quantity of resources to R&D, we would expect continued growth of GDP to result.

4.3 Innovation Diversity

Innovation comes in varieties. It may take several forms. The most important classifications are as follows:

1. Routinized vs. nonroutinized innovations
2. Specific vs. general-purpose technology
3. Product vs. process innovations
4. Exogenous vs. endogenous innovations
5. Physical capital technology base vs. human capital and R&D base
6. Innovation based on marketing and organizational competence

Independent nonroutinized innovations can be viewed as dynamic shocks to the static equilibria of Walrasian competitive system. They may involve new products, processes, organizational forms, or markets. Baumol (2002) has discussed three growth-creating properties of nonroutinized innovations as follows:

(a) The cumulative character of many independent innovations, which not only replace old technology but also create new technical knowledge. The spillover effect is thus enhanced, since such innovations increase the economy's store of knowledge capital.
(b) The public good property of such innovation, which implies economies of scope in the generation of technological improvements for a multiplicity of firms. This property also has the adverse effect that it leads to nonoptimal levels of innovation investment. Appropriate public policy is, therefore, needed here to correct this imbalance.
(c) This innovation has accelerator effects so that the innovating sector's output growth helps other sectors grow.

Routinization of innovation helps to reduce uncertainty. A considerable degree of routinization has now become standard in a wide variety of industries such as computer manufacturing, telecommunications, and pharmaceuticals. Routinization also stabilizes profit levels and efficiency. The new entrants then plan to innovate in new areas for creating new and independent innovations to achieve higher level of quasi-monopoly profits. Thus, the innovation race continues due to competitive pressure of the market.

Specific-purpose technologies (SPT) are incremental processes rather than drastic changes. Growth that is driven by GPT is different from growth driven by incremental innovations. GPT has significant scale effects. In many cases long-run productivity growth initiated by GPT is driven by growth in product quality. But a larger economy produces more varieties of products, which require spreading the quality improving R&D effort over a wider range of products. Growth in software technology has made it much easier for GPT to be applied on a wider scale, and recent trend in the information and communication technology suggests that flexible rather than fixed technology would be increasingly adopted by the innovative firms, e.g., flexible manufacturing.

The distinction between product and process innovation is important in that the process innovation has a cumulative long-run effect. New products have a life cycle of a few years, but new processes allow the adaptation and improvement by successive incremental innovations. Companies develop new products through in-house R&D, e.g., Apple iPad and protect their successes with patent. Product innovation models associate innovation with product quality and rely on the diminishing technical opportunity assumption; innovations with the most impact on quality are discovered first whenever possible. This makes further innovations increasingly difficult to achieve. The quality leader seeks to deter entry of new firms using limit pricing strategies. Sengupta and Fanchon (2009) have recently discussed dynamic limit pricing strategies in such a framework of dominant firms. Process innovations include acquisitions of more efficient machinery, equipment, and software and management training for achieving "core competence." The object is to reduce production and distribution costs and thus gain a competitive advantage over rivals. This type of innovation is most common in modern competitive industries.

Exogenous innovation involves technology creation of the type assumed in the Solow model. The basic research process and experimental activities in university or nonprofit agencies are the closest approximation to exogenous innovation. Endogenous innovations are based on market incentives. Firms invest in such innovations with the expectation of earning quasi-monopoly profits. Baumol (2002) has called such innovation as price-sensitive, i.e., they involve reduction of unit costs and prices and capture price-elastic world markets. Endogenous innovation can take several important forms, e.g., improving the quality of intermediate goods, thereby raising the productivity in assembly of final output, learning by doing, and dynamic comparative advantage by which the high-tech products manufactured in one country can be improved as readily by research labs in a foreign country, and finally, applied research intended to develop new products or processes.

Physical capital accumulation and technology improvement have played a significant role in the development of the modern capitalist world. Economic historians have discussed in some detail the role that new technologies played in spurring the industrial revolution. In modern times human capital has played a more dominant role in the high-tech industries today. Human capital may take two forms: One is the creation of ideas behind the technological improvements, and the other is the R&D investment for developing new products or processes. As examples of ideas one may cite Moore's law, which states that the number of transistors that can be packed onto a computer chip doubles approximately every 18 months. Similarly the PC prices fall every 12 months due to the application of new ideas. Large economies of scale in demand reflect the role of new industrial ideas. Human capital in the form of educational attainments has also played a very important role. According to one estimate the improvements in educational attainments in the USA between 1950 and 1993 involving 4 years of schooling on average explain about 30% of the growth of output per hour. The remaining 70% is attributable to the rise in the stock of ideas produced in the USA, France, UK, Germany, and Japan. The R&D investments intended to develop new products, new processes, or organization skills are more specific, and they are substantially smaller than investment in physical capital, which is often five to ten times larger. Does this mean that R&D investment is less important? Helpman (2004) cited two reasons why it is not so. First, the rate of return on such R&D investment is many times higher than that of physical capital investments in machines and equipment, and second because whenever R&D increases total factor productivity (TFP) (i.e., the upward shift of the production frontier), the higher TFP level induces larger capital accumulation. Some examples of this feedback effect are provided by the growth experience of the fastest growing NICs in Asia. Cost reduction due to R&D investments, which are largely fixed costs, has some very important implications for the industry performance. One implication is that the market structure is likely to be more concentrated, thus affecting the output and price strategies. The second consequence is the externality problem generating spillover benefits. These benefits cannot be internalized by the innovating firms, and hence, there is need for some appropriate public policy. Spence (1984) has discussed this policy framework in his model where R&D investments benefit firms in two ways: One is from accumulation experience of their own R&D, and the other benefit is from the competition itself, i.e., unit costs of R&D decline as the number of firms increases.

Finally, we may refer to innovation in market and organization skills, where creating and expanding markets have helped firms grow by exploiting economies of scale. Introduction of new products generally involves the creation and expansion of new markets, e.g., iPod, iPhone. Market innovation allows the diffusion process to spread new information about the new product. Imitation and improvement are twin objectives for new product and technology markets. Schumpeterian thesis of "creative destruction" can be equally applied to new markets. Old market associated with the old technology or old product declines due to the competitive pressure, and this is replaced by new and larger market associated with the new product. Recent trend in globalization of markets has enhanced the role of dynamic markets in international trade.

4.4 Innovation Policy

The Spence model considers the appropriability problem of an innovating firm, which is large and concentrated and incurs large R&D investments. Since such investments are largely fixed costs, it reduces unit costs, but the spillover benefits cannot all be internally appropriated by the firm. If the R&D for the single firm is not appropriable, the initial incentives to do the R&D investment are reduced. But the price of the output of R&D is close to equal to marginal cost, which may be nearly zero. The marginal cost is the cost of transmitting it to other firms. Thus, there is an unpleasant trade-off between incentives on the one hand and the efficiency with which the industry achieves the level of cost reduction on the other. The most direct way to deal with the problem as suggested by Spence (1984) is to subsidize the R&D activity for which the market provides suboptimally low incentives and has the added benefit of lowering entry barriers, increasing competition, and improving allocation efficiency. Also it makes the industry level more efficient.

Another policy problem arises when the dynamic R&D investment for process innovation occurs in a Cournot duopoly framework, where firms may either undertake independent ventures or form a cartel for cost-reducing R&D investments. In the short run unit costs decline due to R&D and its spillover, but in the long run unit costs rise due to diminishing returns to the fixed R&D capital. The dynamic Cournot model has been formulated by Cellini and Lambertini (2009) along this line, and they have compared the profit and welfare effects of these two settings, i.e., independent R&D labs and joint labs as cartels. They found that private and social incentives toward R&D cooperation coincide for all admissible levels of technological spillovers associated with the innovative activity in the sense that cartelization dominates competition from both standpoints. Also, they found that the larger the extent of technological spillover, the larger the present value of investment efforts over time under both regimes. But the production costs turn out to be smaller under the cooperative agreement. Thus, their model derives the important point that in terms of discounted profits and the value of consumer surplus over time, the conflict between the individual and social incentive is far from being the rule.

Two comments are in order here. One relates to the social welfare viewpoint and the other to the interaction between firms. In the first case, firms form a cartel by choosing output levels noncooperatively while maximizing joint profits with respect to R&D efforts. On comparing with the results from the Spence model, it appears that the cartel framework is more beneficial from a social-welfare viewpoint, and hence, this justifies appropriate state policies. Also, the cost interdependence of firms raises important problems of appropriabilities and externalities, which are not analyzed in this model.

These models, however, ignore an important reason for voluntary dissemination through mutual exchange of technology knowledge. If a firm supplies its technology to a rival and the favor is reciprocated, both firms will end up more strengthened relative to a third competitor. Because of this market forces tend to provide a strong incentive for the formation of informal technology consortia. In many successful NICs of Southeast Asia, industrial parks, export zones, and technology consortia have been deliberately sponsored by the state as a sharing center of new knowledge on the latest technology and software. This may provide one of the most economic ways of solving the externality and spillover problem.

Chapter 5
Diffusion

Diffusion of physical and human capital has played a key role in modern economic growth. Diffusion has three interrelated features. One is the interdependence and linkage of firms, industries, and sectors. The second is the spillover effect and spread of any growth impulse. The third is the cluster effect and agglomeration phenomena by which firms adopt innovating practices. All the three aspects of diffusion stimulate economic growth through productivity increase, market expansion through international trade and knowledge diffusion. According to Helpman (2004), productivity growth of physical and human capital accounts for more than half the variation in growth rates across income per capita countries. Market expansion through trade provides an important mechanism for the international transmission of growth effects. The successful NICs in Southeast Asia provide an important example of this transmission effect. The high growth rates achieved by these countries in the last three decades were largely due to cumulative export growth and dynamic learning by doing methods that generated significant scale economies. Knowledge diffusion occurs through organization learning, exchange of R&D information, and foreign direct investment. Technology transfer by multinational companies (MNCs) has played a key role in the international diffusion of technical knowledge. Joint ventures and cooperation in R&D activities are also important in this connection.

5.1 Technology Transfer

Technology, its knowledge and application can be transferred from one country to another in several forms. It can be transferred in terms of tangible assets such as new products, plant, and equipment and into intangible forms through formal mechanisms such as patents and licenses and informally through information and knowledge flows. Knowledge combines the process of learning with the actual implementation, which involves a shift from the individual level to the widely diffusing competence throughout the whole organization. The spread of information and communication technologies (ITCs) made the process of knowledge diffusion much easier for the MNCs operating across national borders. By the early 1980s, the major MNCs actively sought to

J. Sengupta, *Understanding Economic Growth: Modern Theory and Experience*,
DOI 10.1007/978-1-4419-8026-7_5, © Springer Science+Business Media, LLC 2011

improve transborder knowledge and information flows in the research and design process through the use of new ICTs and software tools. A number of them have integrated their global R&D units via the use of such ICTs and have overcome the need for spatial proximity. Regardless of what type of technology is being transferred, there is always a learning process involved here for subsidiary operations as they become more skilled at adopting and developing new technologies. Overtime MNCs have been increasingly faced with transferring "softer" forms of technology and knowledge as the subsidiaries have matured. An important operation for the MNCs is called "global switching", where they have to consider the location of research and technical activity. Consider an example such as Hewlett Packard, an MNC that displays the phenomenon of global switching in global product development and production. Recently, Nachum (2002) and others have discussed a fundamental change in international business where the MNCs have played a dominant role. Also, mergers and acquisitions at the international level have expanded the market size of high-tech firms today. Developed economies today have undergone a structural transformation from large-scale material manufacturing to designing, networking, and using of new technologies, which operate under increasing returns to scale. Developments in software technology and information networking through knowledge capital have generated significant scale economies. Learning by doing and growth of productivity have usually followed the scale effect. Learning by doing is usually modeled by viewing productivity as an exponential function of cumulative experience. The immediate effect of such productivity growth is the decline in unit costs and prices. This enhances the market and helps through the innovating firm taking advantage of dynamic comparative advantage in international trade.

The link between the propensity of MNCs to operate overseas and their technological skill is well established in international management literature. The IR impact of knowledge-intensive products such as computer hardware and software, telecommunications, and bioengineering drugs has allowed the MNCs to be flexible in their organizational structure. Their ability to successfully establish and maintain network linkages provided a major source of comparative advantage for the MNCs competing in IR industries.

Nachum (2002) used panel data of 390 multinational firms in the USA during 1989–1998 for exhibiting increasing returns to explain FDI flows in terms of several explanatory variables such as innovation capabilities, scale, firm size, and a measure of firm's flexibility. The most significant linear regression coefficients (i.e. 1% level of significance) were found as follows:

Innovation capability	15550.9
Scale	0.199
Multinationality	49710.6
External purchase	72671.5
Adj. R^2	0.755

The strong explanatory power of these variables shows the importance of IR activity and international trade in stimulating US foreign direct investment. The US investment in China, India, and other NICs in the industries based on information technology is largely driven by the profit motive. Of these explanatory variables, the scale economies are very important. It seems that knowledge capital is a complementary nonrivalrous input, helping other inputs grow in productivity.

The MNCs have adopted, however, strategies in many developed and developing countries, which have acted as tacit barriers to entry by domestic firms and this has raised some controversy over MNC's investment in these countries. Dynamic models of limit pricing discuss such strategies of dominant firms and it is necessary for the MNCs to modify their strategies so that some cooperative venture may be adopted.

5.2 Learning by Doing

Knowledge diffusion is more important than technology diffusion, since it allows interdependencies across countries and industries through the spillover effect. In addition, it has the learning-by-doing impact through basic and applied knowledge. Three forms of knowledge diffusion will be discussed here. One is its impact on international trade, which facilitates specialization and, therefore, economies of scale. The second is the learning-by-doing effect, where cumulative experience raises productivity in the firm and the industry as a whole. The third is the R&D effect in industrial countries, which helps the developing economies through externalities, and these benefits are larger when measured in terms of consumption rather than GDP because higher levels of R&D expenditure in the industrial countries bring about significant terms of trade improvement in the less-developed economies. Terms of trade movements provide an important mechanism for the international transmission of growth effects.

Learning by doing is usually measured by cumulative experience proxied by knowledge capital. It is typically formulated as a positive effect of cumulative output and an industry's total factor productivity (TFP). Helpman (2004) discussed this effect by an example as follows.

> To see how learning by doing affects specialization, trade and growth, imagine a country that produces two products, with learning by doing taking place in each of them. The available resources cannot be expanded, implying that productivity is the only viable source of growth. Also suppose that initially the country does not trade with the outside world. Then TFP rises in every sector at a rate that depends on the sector's output level and the sector-specific speed of learning. A sector with faster learning experiences faster growth of its stock of knowledge and fast TFP growth.

R&D investments play a key role in organizational learning. Japan utilized this learning mechanism very successfully while competing with the USA. If there is one country that has challenged the USA for international industrial leadership in the last half of the twentieth century, that country is Japan. In 1950, Japan's GDP per capita was only 20% of that of the USA, but in 1992, it was 90%. Now it is equal or more. The Japanese challenge had come moreover not in those industries in which the US companies were weak. On the contrary, the challenge came in industries such as automobiles, electronics, computers, and machine tools in which the USA attained a leading position. Recent growth experience of NICs in the USA is repeating Japan's role.

Several dynamic features of R&D investment by firms are important for industry growth. First, R&D expenditures not only generate new knowledge about the production process and new products but also enhance the firm's ability to assimilate, exploit, and improve existing knowledge capital. Cohen and Levinthal (1989) have argued that one of the main reasons why firms invest in R&D in the semiconductor industry was that it provides an in-house technical capability that could keep these firms on the leading edge of the latest technology and thereby facilitate the assimilation of new technology developed elsewhere. A second aspect of R&D investment within a firm is its spillover effect. It means that very often this spillover generates "contagion" effects, i.e., knowledge spread this way finds new applications both locally and globally, thereby stimulating further innovative activity in other firms. Finally, the possibility of implicit or explicit collaboration in R&D networking and joint ventures increases the incentive for firms to invest more. Thus, most of the leading software companies in the USA have opened up joint R&D centers or subsidiaries in India. European and Japanese firms are also getting involved.

While R&D investment helps the process of organizational learning, the growth of human capital in the form of general education makes an important contribution to economic growth. For example, the World Bank Report for 1993 found that the proxy measure such as the enrollments in primary education in 1960 predicted the following proportion of economic growth over the period 1960–1985 for the NICs in Asia:

	Growth (%)
Hong Kong	86
Indonesia	79
Japan	58
S. Korea	67
Malaysia	73
Taiwan	69
Singapore	75
Thailand	87

These results are remarkable. They show that the accumulated and improving human capital stock of the Asian NICs contributed to their ability to adopt and endogenize the ever-expanding pool of "best practice" technological knowledge being created at the world level.

Sengupta (2004) analyzed in some detail the role of industrial R&D investment in the computer industry over the period 1987–1998 and found a significant contribution of R&D to the output growth. More recently, Sengupta and Neogi (2009) applied a two-stage model for measuring dynamic efficiency in the US computer industry. In the first stage, the efficient levels of R&D inputs are determined by a nonparametric Pareto-efficiency model otherwise known as data envelopment analysis (DEA) model, and in the second stage, we estimate by a regression model the impact of R&D on total output, proxied by total sales. Our empirical application is based on Standard and Poor's Compustat data for 40 computer firms over the 16-year period 1985–2000. This data set includes such well-known firms as Apple, Dell, IBM, HP, Hitachi, and Toshiba. The linear regression for the efficient firms appears as follows:

$$y = 70.8 + 0.621R + 0.291K + 1.17X,$$
$$R^2 = 0.981,$$

where y is output, R is R&D expenditure, K is net capital expenditure, and X denotes all other direct production inputs. The coefficients for R and K are statistically significant at the 1% level. When the regressions are run separately for the DEA efficient and inefficient firms, the coefficient for R&D inputs is about 12% higher for the efficient firms, while the other coefficients are about the same. When each variable is considered in incremental form, the coefficient for R&D turns out to be 0.65 with $R^2 = 0.994$. It is clear that the R&D input has a very significant marginal contribution to output. When we consider the R&D efficient firms only and several subperiods, the regression results consistently show the dominant role of R&D in its impact on output. The elasticity of output with respect to R&D inputs estimated at the mean level comes out to 0.799 in 1985–1988 and 0.421 in 1985–2000.

5.3 Diffusion Models

Models of diffusion of technology and knowledge deal with the process by which innovation spreads from one firm to another or from one sector to another. The following aspects of these processes will be discussed here:

1. A model of Marshallian diffusion process due to Metcalfe (1994) which treats the diffusion of new technology replacing the old,
2. A model of interaction of knowledge capital in a firm with spillover effects or other firms,
3. A stochastic birth and death process model, where the birth and death rate parameters determine the growth path of creative R&D, and
4. A model of winning the R&D race on the quality ladder due to Folster and Trofimov (1997), where the knowledge spillover stimulates further innovative activity by other firms.

The Marshallian diffusion process model is based on three behavioral premises. One is that output growth of the innovative firm is proportional to the profitability of the new technology subject to the constraint that the unit cost depends on the scale of production of the new technology. The constant of proportion is the diffusion parameter. The higher the diffusion rule of the new technology, the greater the output growth. Second, if demand rises overtime and the new technology has a forward looking view of market growth, it stimulates growth of capacity. Finally, the learning curve effect here implies declining unit costs through increase in cumulative output and/or the spillover diffusion effect. Under some standard assumptions, these premises generate a logistic growth path of output under the equilibrium. Metcalfe has drawn two important implications from this solution path. One is that during the diffusion process, if one solves for the equilibrium prices where price equals marginal cost, then it is more profitable to adopt the new over the old one. Second, the time path of relative substitution of the new technology replacing the old also follows a logistic curve. But since the diffusion parameters are not all deterministic in the long run, their stochastic variations imply a nonlogistic substitution curve. Stochastic variations in the diffusion and technology adoption parameters are very basic to the Schumpeterian growth model, which explains how the innovation flow develops out of the new initiative of the innovative entrepreneurs, how it generates rents and monopoly profits, and how it aids the process of dispersal across industries and international markets.

A linear birth and death process model discussed in some detail by Sengupta (2004) contains two positive parameters: b for the birth rate and d for the death rate, where their difference $g=b-d$ determines the exponential growth or decay of R&D investment. These parameters can be interpreted differently in different frameworks. Also the growth path of R&D investment would generate a long-run growth path of output in equilibrium assuming an expanding market. The linear birth and death process model may easily characterize the Schumpeterian innovation process as a two-stage process, where the flow of innovations in technology and new knowledge constitute the first stage followed by the process of what is called "creative destruction." The first type formulates a stochastic flow model for innovation input in the form of knowledge capital. Here both may denote the creation of new ideas and death the relative obsolescence or destruction of the old. Then the second stage formulates a dynamic adjustment model for the successful innovator, who is assumed to minimize a loss function based on the discounted stream of deviations of innovative inputs from their desired or target levels. Clearly when the birth rate exceeds the death rate, $g=b-d$ is positive and the innovation process in then unbounded. The resulting output process then exhibits increasing returns and this framework is most appropriate for modern high-tech industries such as computers and telecommunications industries.

A more general form of the linear birth and death process model occurs when the two parameters b and d change overtime generating a nonlinear process. If the birth rate parameter declines with the innovation output, while the death rate remains proportional to output, this framework generates a logistic growth model, where the upper asymptote indicates a steady state. This steady state continues till a new innovator ushers in a new innovation displacing the old. This type of nonlinear stochastic model has been generalized by Sengupta (2004) for a two-sector framework, where one innovating firm is more productive than the other. The first sector may then play a more dominating role like the leader follower model in the Cournot-Nash framework.

An interesting application of the birth and death process model arises when the birth rate is interpreted as an infection rate affecting the other sectors. The contagion effect then describes an evolutionary process. This contagion effect is very similar to the concept of "forward linkage" in development theory. When there is a spillover of knowledge and technology, this contagion parameter may take higher values indicating a stronger interdependence impact.

Recent empirical studies have shown that the R&D investment generating new knowledge in the USA and other developed countries has spread to the developing countries, and the NICs in Southeast Asia have taken full advantage. Many incremental innovations that come in small steps, e.g., in software and other communication fields, have generated new improvements in further innovations in these NICs, and this is evident by their boom *n* exports of the technology-intensive products and processes. The opening of subsidiaries and joint ventures for the innovating firms in the USA and Europe also confirm the same trend.

Finally, we discuss the model of industry evolution through R&D spillover effects and externalities due to Folster and Trofimov. This model assumes that R&D externalities generate increasing returns to scale for the whole industry, since knowledge acquired in one firm spills over to other firms. But the winner of the R&D race is successful in improving the quality ladder and hence it increases the price exactly to the extent of the quality improvement. But the other competitors are nonleaders behaving as Bertrand followers. As the price increases, the winning leader firm becomes a monopoly producer. This model generates multiple equilibria, some of which are stable and some are unstable. An empirical application of this model to 82 R&D projects in the Swedish industry over 1988–1990 involving about 7% of total private R&D spending in Sweden showed that there can be ranges of aggregate increasing returns to research in which an industry can converge in different equilibria. Furthermore, the empirical regression indicated that the education level, technological competence, and past sales increase a country's chance of being the base for new firms or new MNCs.

5.4 Incremental Diffusion

Like innovation, the diffusion process is rarely the dramatic breakthroughs that Schumpeter may have had in mind, but are rather small improvements and small dispersal of a new process or product in which novelty and imitation with a difference shade imperceptibly into one another. Two aspects of this incremental diffusion associated with the incremental innovations have to be noted. One is the nature of technological knowledge characterized by Aghion and Howitt as quoted by Baumol (2002) as follows:

> Technical knowledge is itself a kind of capital good. It can be used in combination with other factors of production to produce final output. It can be stored overtime because it does not get completely used up whenever it is put into a production process and it can be accumulated through R&D and other knowledge–creation activities, a process that involves the sacrifice of current resources in exchange for future benefits. In all these respects knowledge is just a kind of disembodies capital good.

The second aspect of incremental diffusion is "the diffusion of knowledge," which is closely related to the concept of the division of labor. To Hayek goes the credit of emphasizing the concept of division of knowledge as central to the growth of industrial capitalism. The division of labor, which is the heart of specialization and economies of scale, is the primary means of increasing the division of knowledge and thereby of promoting the growth of knowledge. Growth of knowledge and its industry-wide spread is a key element in long-term growth, and collaboration is one of the most important means of fostering innovation and its dispersal through knowledge division. Some empirical aspects of this process may be worth mentioning. We may refer here to the Cambridge University's ESRC Center for Business Research (CBR) Survey reports for 1991, 1993, and 1995 which analyzed data for 2,028 firms, both innovating and noninnovating. Small firms depended more on incremental innovation rather than dramatic ones. Overall, the innovating firms stressed the importance of higher-order qualitative factors that require investment in skills and technical capability. The reports concluded that one of the most important ingredients for achieving competitive success appears to be to establish effective collaboration with others, e.g., customers, suppliers, higher education establishments, and so on. Such collaboration allowed firms to expand their range of expertise, develop and improve specialized products and processes. In terms of percentage of respondents, the following factors of competitive advantage may be noted in particular:

	All	Innovators	Noninnovators
Product quality	85.2	87.6	78.9
Specialized expertise	83.4	82.7	84.9
Speed of service	75.2	73.5	79.9
Cost advantage	34.3	33.8	34.9

Nearly half of the innovating firms in the CBR survey had entered into collaborative partnership, whereas only one in six of the noninnovating firms had entered into such arrangements. Also the survey found that collaboration is particularly important for firms facing foreign competition. The current trend in globalization of markets is sure to intensify this collaborative strategy for incremental knowledge diffusion process.

There is an apparent conflict between the incremental innovation and its diffusion. If a firm incurs huge expenditure for its innovation program, e.g., pharmaceutical and computer industries, but finds that other firms including its rivals share in the fruits, why should the innovating firm devote time, effort and funding to continue that program? Baumol (2002) has mentioned two incentive mechanisms.

One is that both the proprietor of the new technology or knowledge and the renter getting the license may gain from such a transfer just as it occurs in international trade theory as comparative advantage and gains from trade. A firm that holds the rights to a valuable innovation is in the same position of that which owns a facility with abundant capacity and superior quality. The renter for the new technology license may be willing to pay a higher remunerative price than the return the owner could have obtained by using the new technology in its own operation. The purchasers of such licenses are willing to pay a higher price because such friendly and voluntary transfer of technology is substantially more rapid than "hostile transfers" through industrial espionage and reverse engineering. This is because rapid obsolescence makes speed in providing the latest model so critical in high-tech industries today. A second incentive for licensing of new technology and new knowledge is that this process can help the innovating firms to help at least partly to internalize the externalities of innovation activity.

An important element of incremental innovation in the form of R&D investment is the economies of scale and also scope. R&D expenditures exceed 5% of total sales at many high-tech companies such as Intel, Microsoft, GlaxoSmithKline, and GE. The pharmaceutical companies spend upwards of $500 million to successfully develop a new drug. There is a substantial indivisible investment, implying that every fixed cost will decline very rapidly as the sales of the drug increase. The implication for profit is apparent. R&D expenditures may also entail economies of scope, if ideas developed in one research project create positive spillovers to another project. By using detailed R&D data, Henderson and Cockburn (1996) analyzed the evidence of scope economies in the pharmaceutical firms. By using the number of patents per dollar of R&D as a measure of productivity, they found that an average firm with 19 research programs was 4.5% more productive than a firm with 17 programs. Large firms may benefit from spillovers but smaller firms may have greater incentive to innovate. Moreover, the smaller firms may take a variety of independent approaches to tackling research problems. Such a strategy increases the probability of success of smaller firms in incremental innovation and its diffusion.

Finally, one should note that the paradigm of incremental innovation depends on the market for new ideas. This market expands through incremental diffusion of ideas. This market is highly competitive and global in size. This is a network of communications. The more it expands, the more scale economies it generates and more the innovating firm gains by selling its new technology license. Teece (1986) has identified two elements of this market for ideas: (1) non-expropriation of technology by others because of low spillover effect and (2) specialized assets or skills such as marketing capabilities. When the possibility for expropriation is high, the innovating firm has two options. One is to create barriers to entry if possible. The second is to enter into some venture or collaborative arrangement on the R&D side, so that some externalities may be shared. Teece's second point is that innovative products must be produced and marketed. If many firms have the required expertise in production and marketing, they will compete for the rights to the innovation or for getting the technology license thus leaving most of the profits to the innovator.

But if the required expertise is scarce, the innovator can no longer sell to the highest bidder. To consider an example of this situation, one may refer to the case to a California biotech firm Celtrix, which held valuable patents on a cell regulating protein that would heal damaged cells. Although Celtrix developed the protein, Celtrix had to enter joint venture arrangements on terms favorable to Genentech to get the rights to use the patented process.

Finally, we conclude with Baumol's comment on incremental innovation and its diffusion as follows:

> One reason for voluntary dissemination is that proprietary technology is like any other asset in this respect – it is profitable to rent it out if the price is right. After all, if the price is sufficiently high, employment of its technology by others will be the most profitable option to the owner. And it will pay the prospective renter to offer such an attractive price whenever it is in a position to put the technology to better use than the proprietor. As a result, it is not surprising that substantial markets in technology licenses have emerged.

5.5 Concluding Remarks

In conclusion, we may note some world perspective. Technology in various forms is created in response to market pressure. Research and development resources are concentrated in rich countries led by global corporations. In 1998, the 29 OECD countries spent $520 billion on R&D – more than the combined economic output of the world's 30 poorest countries. OECD countries with 19% of the world's people also accounted for 91% of the 347,000 net patents issued in 1998. And in these countries, more than 60% of R&D is carried on by the private sector. As a result research neglects to develop technologies for poor people. Technology is also unevenly diffused across the world. OECD countries contain 79% of the world's internet users. The global map of technological achievement in modern times shows huge inequalities between countries – not only in terms of innovation and access but also in the education and skills required to use technology actively. Technology is also unevenly diffused within countries. India is a home to a world-class technology hub in Bangalore but ranks at the lower end of the technology achievement index prepared by the UNDP. Why? Because Bangalore is a small enclave in a country where the average adult received only 5.1 years of education, adult illiteracy is around 44%, and the electricity consumption is about half that in China.

In this network age, every country needs the capacity to understand and adapt global technologies for local needs. Lack of this capacity is one potent source of world income inequality. Widespread technology diffusion is the key to reduce such inequality.

Chapter 6
Asian Miracles

High and sustained economic growth of eight Asian economies such as Japan, Hong Kong, South Korea, Singapore, Taiwan, Indonesia, Malaysia, and Thailand during the period of 1965–1990 is characterized as a growth miracle by the World Bank Report (1993). The above mentioned eight high-performing Asian economies (HPAEs) had experienced rapid and sustained growth over the period of 1960–1990 and thereafter, and their experience is unique in combining rapid growth with highly equal income distribution. This study regressed per capita economic growth in terms of eight explanatory variables such as relative GDP 1960, primary-school enrollment 1960, secondary-school enrollment 1960, population growth 1960–1985, average ratio of investment to GDP 1960–1985, dummy variables for HPAEs, Latin America, and Sub-Saharan Africa and the respective coefficients turned out to be –0.032*, 0.027**, 0.007, 0.100, 0.028, 0.017**, –0.013**, –0.010*. The adjusted R^2 is 0.482, and the one and two asterisks denote statistical significance at 5 and 1% respectively. Rodrick (1994) excluded the investment rate, secondary education, and the population growth rate, which were not statistically significant, and included the Gini coefficient for inequality in land ownership 1960 and in income distribution 1960; the coefficients turned out to be as follows:

Relative GDP (1960)	–0.38*
Primary-school enrollment (1960)	2.66**
Gini coefficient for land (1960)	–5.22**
Gini coefficient for income (1960)	–3.47
Adjusted R^2	0.53

On taking the Asian countries as a group, there is a significantly lower degree of inequality in land and income distribution than in other less-developed countries. Thus, Rodrick's findings suggest that less inequality in land distribution is associated with higher economic growth.

Two sources of this miracle are identified by the World Bank study: accumulation of physical and human capital and the productivity change. Productivity change is measured by total factor productivity (TFP) growth, which is estimated in a simple neoclassical framework by subtracting from output growth the portion

J. Sengupta, *Understanding Economic Growth: Modern Theory and Experience*,
DOI 10.1007/978-1-4419-8026-7_6, © Springer Science+Business Media, LLC 2011

of growth due to capital accumulation, human capital accumulation (primary education enrollment level as a proxy), and labor force growth. On using data for 87 high-to-low income economies the resulting estimates for TFP for the HPAEs (1960–1989) are as follows:

Hong Kong	3.647	Indonesia	1.254
Japan	3.478	South Korea	3.102
Singapore	1.190	Taiwan	3.760
Thailand	3.760	Malaysia	1.075
Latin America	0.127	Africa	−0.998

Another fundamental characteristic of the East-Asian success story is that depending on the estimates used about 60–120% of their output growth derives from accumulation of physical and human capital and labor force growth. One should mention two other important sources of rapid growth. One is maintaining competitive efficiency in the export market and openness of international trade. Learning by doing and developing joint ventures with international firms helped significantly. One of the keys to success of the export push in some of the HPAEs especially Japan, South Korea, and Taiwan was the government's ability to combine cooperation with competition. Another important source of rapid growth is to maintain macroeconomic stability by well-designed fiscal and monetary policy. Sequencing of the leading industries in the economy has also been emphasized by the World Bank study as a key for rapid growth. For example the industrial policy in Japan has been centered on promoting industry after industry: from textiles and toys, steel, chemicals, shipbuilding to high-tech industries. Taiwan concentrated on computers, software, and R&D designs. It developed light and low-tech industries and then jumped to the next stage, the mid-tech industries. Today it is competing in the high-tech fields.

We may now discuss some specific country episodes as follows:

1. China's experience
2. India and China
3. Taiwan and Korea
4. Learning by doing and efficiency growth

The growth experience of the NICs in Asia is unique in many ways. Compared to Africa and Latin America their average growth rates over the last three decades have been high and self-sustained. China's experience has been most significant along with Taiwan and South Korea.

6.1 China's Experience

The three most important features of China's rapid growth experience are (1) productivity and efficiency growth (2) openness in international trade and support for FDI and (3) fast rate of restructuring the industry structure. Recently Wu (2008) has econometrically estimated productivity growth in China by a stochastic frontier function. He has examined he sources of economic growth, i.e., input changes and the magnitude of the residual often called TFP growth. Three earlier estimates are as follows.

		Contributions (%)			
	Growth (%)	K	L	TFP	Total
World Bank (1997) 1978–1995	9.4	37	17	46	100
Bosworth and Collins (2003) 1980–1990	9.2	23	31	46	100
Bosworth and Collins (2003) 1990–2000	10.3	32	18	50	100

Wang and Yao (2003) separated the impact of human capital from TFP growth and thus obtained a TFP share of about 25%. Here K is physical capital, L is labor, and TFP is total factor productivity. Wu (2008) decomposed output growth by the stochastic frontier estimate as follows.

	1983–1991	1992–2000	2001–2004
ICT Capital	−0.21	4.37	2.65
	(−2.5)	(46.1)	(24.7)
Other capital	5.58	5.58	5.2
	(69.3)	(55.1)	(56.1)
Labor	1.58	0.39	0.39
	(19.6)	(4.1)	(3.6)
TFP	1.10	−0.51	1.66
	(13.6)	(−5.3)	(15.5)
Output	8.75	9.49	10.70
	(100.0)	(100.0)	(100.0)

Figures in parenthesis are the shares of growth components. Here total physical capital is decomposed into two components: information and communications technology (ICT) and other capital. Other capital includes all other forms of physical capital inputs other than ICT employed in the production process. Technology or TFP is derived as the residual of an aggregate production function. The estimates are as given above. Another estimate obtained by Wu (2008) decomposed sources of growth by FTP, technical efficiency (TE), and scale efficiency (SE) as follows.

	Sources of growth		
	1993–1997	1998–2000	2001–2004
	Average annual rate		
TFP	1.64	4.30	3.56
TE	−0.26	1.89	1.19
SE	1.16	0.62	0.80
Output	12.40	8.99	10.95
TFP/output	13.23	47.81	32.47

Several important points emerge from Wu's study. Overall the TFP growth accounts for about 27% of the total growth in the Chinese economy over the period of 1993–2004. Wu's conclusion is that there is further scope for gains in TFP in the recent period. Second, the estimates of contribution of ICT capital turns out to be 4.37 during 1992–2000 and 2.65 during 2001–2004, and this estimate is based on an assumed depreciation rate of 15% for the ICT capital. These results differ from those of previous studies. For example Wang and Yao (2003) estimate that TFP contributed 25% to economic growth and total capital accumulation (both ICT and non-ICT capital) contributed to half of economic growth. In another study by Qian and Smyth (2006) that includes human capital as a separable factor input, TFP and human capital contribute 22 and 13% of total GDP growth, respectively.

China's productivity growth largely resulted from efficiency gains associated with economic reforms, which included openness in international trade. The reforms also brought about reallocation of resources from agricultural to the manufacturing and ICT sectors. Also it involved large-scale diversion of capital and know-how from state enterprises to the private sector. China's technical advance has also helped the growth of investment in education and R&D expenditure in the last three decades. However, China still lags behind substantially in its spending on R&D and education. For example most OECD countries spend twice as much as China does on R&D activities. A UN Report (2004) shows the following percentages of R&D and education expenditures over GDP.

	R&D exp (2001)	Education (2000)	HDI rank (2003)
US	2.8	4.8	10
Singapore	2.1	3.3	25
South Korea	3.0	3.8	28
Mexico	0.4	4.4	53
Malaysia	0.4	6.2	61
China	1.1	2.9	85

Note that other successful NICs in Asia such as Korea and Singapore spend much more than China. These countries do much better in terms of the HDI measure. But the future trend looks brighter as the policy makers in China are determined to follow the target of making China the hub of technological progress in the world. As Wu (2008) has concluded:

> It can be anticipated that investment in R&D and education in China will keep growing in the future. This growth will come from both the public and private sectors. Potential policy initiatives would include the development of a venture investment market, establishment of the science and technology market, introduction of R&D bonds and incentives for the promotion indigenous R&D activities. The implementation of these initiatives would further boost spending on innovation and hence productivity growth in China.

One must discuss now two most important aspects of Chinese economic reforms which generated rapid growth episodes. One is the rural economic reform since 1978. Rural industries have received special attention in the development literature because they are key to the industrialization process, and they help in the process of equitable distribution of income. China has attracted considerable attention for its radical rural collectivization policies for the first three decades after the communists came to power and its relatively high growth rates. The other important feature of economic reform policies is the financial sector reforms. The success of the grand Chinese transition to a market-oriented economy crucially depends on China's success in developing a sound and efficient financial system. By joining the World Trade Organization (WTO) by the end of 2001, China agreed to liberalize its trade and foreign investment, as well as implementing a phased opening of its financial system to foreign capital investment and joint ventures. We would now discuss these features of Chinese economic reforms.

In the making of the East-Asian Growth Miracle, there are two variants. One is the group consisting of Japan, Korea, and Taiwan, the other is China. The first group experienced rapid transformation from rural to urban based on industry rather than agriculture as their main source of income. This industrialization process maintained a healthy agricultural sector, which helped to arrest more inequality of income distribution. The development episode in China over the last three decades started with off-farm work emerging as a main source of income growth for many rural households. Recently Huang et al. (2006) have analyzed this growth process in its several important aspects. The first aspect deals with China's reform period (1979–1995) when the rapid and monotonic expansion of the real output of major food crops ranked as one of the nation's great successes. Thus, rice production increased by 20%, wheat by 80%, and maize by 95% during the 1980s and early 1990s. Second, they estimated TFP growth for the three major crops: rice, wheat, and maize during 1979–1995; in general China's TFP has risen at a healthy rate of 2% per year during the reform period. In the late reform period of 1984–1995 technology remained the most important source of TFP growth. China's crop breeding technology developed by the agricultural scientists has helped enhance the quality of its seed stock. Since China started its plant biotechnology program in the mid-1980s, it has grown fast and has taken a steady path of expansion. Almost all plant biotechnology research is funded by the government policy. According to one estimate China's total investment in plant biotechnology in 1999 was about $112 million in US dollars. It has increased steadily over the recent years.

Another way to analyze the Chinese rural economy is to divide the overall rural economy into two sectors, namely, the agricultural sector and the rural small-scale enterprises (RSE) sector ortownship and village enterprises (TVE), and then analyze their growth pattern over the reform period and thereafter. Sengupta and Lin (1993) estimated that the RSE sector in 1976 accounted for 23.3% of total rural output and 5% of the total rural labor force, but in 1987 these shares rose to 47 and 20.9%, respectively. During 1990–2006 these exceeded 65 and 45% respectively. Sengupta and Lin divided the Chinese rural economy into three regions: high-income, middle-income, and low-income regions. The high-income region consists of eight provinces: Shanghai, Beijing, Tianjing, Liaoning, Guandong, Jiansu, Zhejiang, and Shangdong. The middle-income region includes 13 provinces: Hebei, Shanxi, and others. The low-income region consists of the rest. The high-income region has the greatest success in generating rural nonagricultural employment opportunities and income growth. The middle-income region contains more than 50% of the total surplus labor force and a very low level of per capita income. In low-income regions such as Gansu and Guizhou provinces, nonagricultural employment in 1980 constituted less than 3% of total rural employment. Sengupta and Lin estimated that for the period of 1978–1990 the average labor productivity of the RSE sector was about 3.6 times higher than that of the agricultural sector and that the RSE sector is found to have a strong positive externality effect on agricultural production. This spillover effect is mainly due to improved learning by doing and more efficient managerial skills. Second, the high- and middle-income regions show strong evidence of increasing returns to scale exceeding 1.05. This trend has continued in recent years 1991–2006, thanks to the market-based incentives and more openness in trade.

Any study of China's rural economy would be incomplete without a study of China's collectives. An important research work in this field is done by Piek (1998) who collected longitudinal statistical data for the period of 1980–1990. This data covered the rural industry in two counties of Santai and Qianwei. The importance of collectives in rural industry and rural manufacturing may be seen from the following data.

	Share of collectives in % of total rural manufacturing	
	Santai	Qianwei
No. of enterprises	10	10
No. of employees	42	51
Fixed capital	91	82
Gross value of output	61	45

These two counties are both densely populated and have a prosperous agricultural sector. In 1990 agriculture was still the major sector in which the skill levels were low. Economic liberalization policies increased the opportunities for employment outside agriculture, which then broadened the skill levels of the labor force in Santai and Quanwei. A second feature of development in these two counties is that the rise of noncollectives has reduced the share of manufacturing in the rural industry and in manufacturing. However, it has not substantially reduced their share in fixed capital.

Two recent policy trends are important. One is the Sparke Programme started by the Chinese government as a means to raise the rural technological level. This program focuses on developing production programs, which should consider local agriculture and the related activities. It is important to note that the government has set up Quality Checking Bureaus and Standard Measure Bureaus to check and improve quality products. For the sample enterprises covered in the study, quality was checked for 68% of the Santai subsample and 31% of the Quanwei subsample. International standards are followed for export products, and recently the government has stepped up the upgrading of quality standards. The other important trend in recent years is to introduce enterprise responsibility. The financial reforms led to less dependence on the government as the only source of finance. The technological environment of the sample enterprises consists of interenterprise and enterprise-institutional relations through which firms are able to acquire and develop their technology. The recent policy reforms have provided ample scope for enterprises to establish their own technological and innovation network. This has recently started a process of widespread broadening of possible sources of technology. China could very well follow Taiwan's model, which thrives under this strategy.

China's transition to a market economy and participation in the competitive world market depends on its success on a sound and efficient financial system. The monetary reform in 1994 transferred the bulk of national banking to three newly created banks (The Long-Term development and Credit Bank, The Import–Export Bank, and the Agricultural Development Bank) and four specialized banks into a state-owned commercial bank (SOCB). The SOCBs were given the government directive to operate according to internationally accepted commercial banking practices. The SOCBs account for about 72% of all outstanding loans in China and nearly 90% in financial intermediation. In addition to these four pillars of China's banking system, over the last decade 1996–2006, many SOCBs were created to meet the financial needs of provinces or special economic zones like the export zones. Local Chinese banks have often been used by the state as a tool for quasi-fiscal operations. Most of the loans were used to sustain the operation of SOEs so as to avoid unemployment. However, the situation has changed drastically since 1995, when Beijing started earnestly to restructure the corporate and banking sectors. Today the state sector accounts for just about 60% of total banking credit, down from 100% in the early 1980s.

China's economic growth has been impressive. Since 1997 the fiscal policy has been the main source of economic growth in China. In addition, over the period of 2000–2004 foreign direct investment geared toward exports has acted as a second important contribution to China's rapid economic growth. Since 1995, exports accounting for roughly 28% of China's GDP have contributed to nearly 41% of its growth, primarily through the industrial sector. Future long-run growth of China depends crucially on the successful implementation of policies designed to promote the nonstate sector. Hence, the development of the financial sector is crucial. Continued development of China's financial system requires interest rate liberalization, capital account convertibility, and increased exchange rate flexibility. Beijing's desire to keep its currency renminbi competitive to attract foreign capital for the purpose of job creation and export promotion is understandable. Yet a gradual process of liberalization is needed for future sustained growth.

A study of average efficiency of 22 commercial banks by Yao et al. (2006) over the period of 1995–2001, when efficiency measured by pretax profits showed that it is quite low at 63%. In the literature, the average efficiency score is about 80% for the US banks. This difference of efficiency estimates is probably due to government control and intervention in China. Many commercial banks in China suffer from the plight of so-called large volume of nonperforming loans (NPLs) resulting from state policy directives. The current competitive system is not good enough for Chinese banks to compete with foreign banks, which have immense financial resources and international expertise.

The banks in China have much to learn from the Korean financial crisis in 1998, which had its roots in a bad banking system. The Korean government played a big role in directing banks to lend to the politically connected chaebol. Easy credit led to a dangerously leveraged corporate sector with a debt–equity ratio of over 500% in most Korean firms, just before the financial crisis broke in 1998. The huge risk of concentration by large and dominant firms aggravated by borrowers' reckless expansion had threatened the viability of the Korean banking system in the era of financial crisis in 1998. China does not have to follow the Korean chaebol model to build world-class manufacturing. Taiwan's development model stands up better. Taiwan's petrochemical and high-tech firms are as successful as the Korean's chaebol. But unlike the Korean giants Taiwan's many small- and mid-sized firms are more flexible, and they have proven to be more resilient to adverse shocks such as the Asian financial crisis.

6.2 India and China

India's growth episode is as important as China for several reasons. It has more than a billion population with a large middle class, which is to grow more than 40%. This has enormous demand potential. Second, it has developed its IT sector and software technology over the last two decades. Foreign direct investment in India has also increased significantly over the last two decades. However, India has many lessons to learn from China and other successful NICs. We consider some of these lessons below.

One of the most important lessons for India is to open up in a steady but cautious fashion. Since 1951 India followed an important substitution policy in international trade, whereas the successful NICs in Asia including China followed an active export promotion (EP) strategy. The final result was that the private investment rate in India was badly constrained by the sluggish domestic agricultural expansion and cut off from the elastic world markets. By contrast the private investment rate in the successful NICs in Asia began to take off to phenomenal levels because East Asia turned to the EP strategy. Three aspects of the EP strategy help step up the growth rate. The first aspect is the forward and backward linkage effects, e.g., the expectation of substantial export earnings induces more investment in importing new equipment and R&D knowledge capital embodying new technical change. The second aspect is the learning-by-doing impact of foreign direct investment. The main reason why the EP strategy worked so well for the Asian NICs is their networking model. China opened up its industry to heavy investment from Taiwan, and Korea's investment was contributed in large part by Japan. Other successful NICs in Asia invited joint ventures with high-tech companies through networking and R&D investments. They were able to capitalize on the R&D spillover effects. The ratio of FDI to GDP rose in China from 0.9% in 1990 to 5.11 in 1997 to 4.08% in 1999. Borensztein and Lee (1998) tested the effect of FDI on economic growth in 69 developing countries over the last two decades using a cross-country regression framework.

Their findings show that FDI is an important channel for the transfer of technology, contributing relatively more to growth than domestic investment. However, they conclude that the higher productivity of FDI holds only when the host country has a minimum stock of human capital. Recently, the econometric estimates by Zheng et al. (2006) based on Chinese panel data over the period of 1985–1999 showed the following regression coefficients of the log of growth of human capital, ratio of FDI to GDP lagged by a year, and the log of growth rate of labor: 0.132, 0.089, and 0.089. The dependent variable is the log of growth rate of GDP. The coefficients are all statistically significant at 1%. The adjusted R^2 varies from 0.192 in the ordinary least squares to 0.346 in the random effects model. These results repeated over the coastal, central, and western regions confirm the hypothesis that China's economic growth has been mainly driven by the expansion of FDI, the labor force, and human capital (learning by doing).

The major thrust of East-Asian development has been the rapid growth of manufacturing. This has involved four major components: (1) zero or low tariffs, (2) implicit or explicit subsidization of exports and (3) export processing zones, and (4) convertibility of currency for current account transactions. This openness in trade has helped improve industry efficiency through importing the latest technology and utilizing it for transmission of growth externalities to other sectors of the domestic economy. This strategy was vigorously followed by China and Taiwan, who energized their medium- and small-scale enterprises and helped create rural employment and income. Sachs et al. (1999) have correlated an openness index with the FDI/GDP ratio in 1994 as follows.

	Openness index	Average tariff rate	FDI/GDP ratio (%)
India	25	33	0.3
China	60	5	5.1
South Korea	55	4	0.2
Malaysia	171	9	8.0

Here the openness index is measured by the share of GDP contributed by total exports and imports. The comparative evidence is self-revealing.

Private consumption has already played a much larger role in India's growth than it has in that of other developing countries. In 2005 private spending reached about 17 trillion Indian rupees ($372 billion in US dollars) accounting for more than 60% of India's GDP. In this respect India is closer to developed economies such as Japan and the USA than are China and other NICs in Asia. One research study estimates that total consumer spending could more than quadruple in coming years, reaching 70 trillion rupees by 2025. This has two major implications for future growth. First, India will attract both domestic and world business. The areas of excellence in the IT sector and software technology would thrive through dynamic increasing returns to scale, and the scope of dynamic comparative advantage would increase. Second, the increase in total consumer spending across regions would need to be decentralized as a consequence of the spillover effects. Like Taiwan and China this should help the knowledge diffusion process.

One of the greatest growth resources of India is the knowledge capital and its potential through population growth. The Human Development Report (2004) by UNDP lists the following statistics for human skills for NICs in Asia.

	Mean years of schooling (2000)	Gross tertiary science enrollment ratio (%)
India	5.1	1.7
China	6.4	3.2
South Korea	10.8	23.2
Singapore	7.1	24.2
Malaysia	6.8	3.3

Clearly China's science enrollment ratio is almost double that of India. India's government spending on public education is about 4.1% of GDP during 1998–2000, while China spends only 2.1%. Yet the performance of rural, small- and medium-sized enterprises in India has been insignificant.

Sengupta (2005) has analyzed the details of the economic performance of the software industry in India and its weaknesses. A growth strategy for the new economy in India has to be viewed in broadest terms as Schumpeterian innovations. These include R&D investment in the traditional sense, new designs in software development, skill development in the technology-intensive sectors, and developing new products and processes for the world market. We may note some encouraging trends in recent years. First, India has started development centers through collaboration with foreign firms catering to overseas software-based business applications. Several locations such as China, Eastern Europe, and others exist for locating outsourcing opportunities, but India is still most popular due to its cost-efficiency and supply of skilled manpower. For example Oracle's facility in India is currently responsible for maintenance of all the application software products.

China's recent policy is striving to push China up the innovation ladder in the next 15 years 2010–2025 by raising R&D spending to 2% of GDP in 2010 and 2.5% in 2020 from the current 1.3% in 2009. That will put China on par with the USA and Germany. This also implies that China's R&D spending will rise at an annual rate of 21% over the medium term, significantly faster than the expected growth rate of GDP of about 11%. There are other long-term efforts stipulated in the Long-term Science and Technology Development Plan for the next 15 years declared by the Chinese government. One is to raise the contribution of productivity from technology improvement to 60% of economic growth by 2020 from less than 40% in 2009 and cut the dependency on imported technologies by half from the current 60% of all technologies used in 2009. Another is to step up the number of patents obtained by China, where Taiwan ranks very close to the USA and other developed nations. The government is also stepping up tax incentives and subsidies to boost innovations in industry in all fields. It will now allow exemption of 150% of R&D spending form the corporate income tax, up from the current 100%. This is especially beneficial for start-up technology firms.

High-tech firms will also be allowed to depreciate their investments in R&D facilities much faster, which means bigger tax-deductibles. Meanwhile, new high-tech setups in designated high-tech development zones will be entitled to a 2-year income tax exemption from the first profit-making year and a favorable rate of 15% afterward. Fiscal spending on R&D is a key initiative to mobilize and induce more private investment. The Long-Term Plan aims at boosting the growth rate of fiscal spending on R&D sharply higher than that of overall government spending. The lessons for Indian government and business are clear. It should make the strongest effort to promote home-grown technologies and the innovation capability of domestic firms in China.

As we discussed before, the success in world markets depends very crucially on the efficiency of the financial system, which comprises banks and related institutions. Recently Sengupta and Neogi (2009) have discussed the performance of the Indian banking sector. The banking sector plays a dynamic role in the growth strategy of an economy by facilitating loans, managing risks, and stimulating international transactions. India initiated financial reforms in the banking sector in 1991 as a part of a broad reform in economic policy. Sengupta and Sahoo (2006) have studied 78 commercial banks in India over the 5-year period of 1997–2001 comprising nationalized, private, and foreign banks. This study applied the Pareto efficiency model known as data envelopment analysis by estimating an efficient production frontier. With three inputs, namely, borrowed funds, labor and fixed assets, and a composite output combining investments and performing loan assets, the production frontier was used to estimate the scale and scope economies and capacity utilization ratio for the sample banks. Three results are most interesting. In terms of scale economies the private banks comprising private and foreign banks perform much better than the state-controlled nationalized banks. Second, it is found that the banking sector in India is characterized by monopolistic competition. Finally, private banks including foreign banks are found to be more efficient in terms of their capacity utilization than the nationalized banks. This excess capacity in the nationalized banking sector seems to imply an increase in cost inefficiency for long-run costs. Clearly there is ample scope of liberalization and reforms in banking policy in India.

6.3 Taiwan and Korea

The growth experiences of Taiwan and South Korea are important in the Asian growth miracle for two reasons. Taiwan is a small country, but it has achieved phenomenal success in the high-tech field. It has also stimulated economic growth in China through significant collaboration and investment. Korea is a larger country than Taiwan and has been helped by Japan through investment and technology transfer.

The growth miracles exhibited by the successful NICs in Asia have been used by Lucas (1993) as examples of the spillover effect and economies of scale due to

R&D and knowledge capital. These economic features are consistently emphasized by the endogenous growth theory. But recently Jones (1995a, b) performed some econometric tests. He proposed two direct tests of endogenous growth. One is that permanent changes in the investment rate have permanent effects on national growth rate, and the second is that R&D expenditures embodying human capital have permanent impact on the economic growth rate.

For the first hypothesis Jones tested the AK model Y = AK of the endogenous growth theory, which predicts that permanent changes in government policies affecting investment rates lead to permanent changes in a country's growth of per capita GDP. This model takes national output (Y) as a linear function of accumulated capital (K), which is broadly defined so as to include both physical capital and human capital. The production function assumes constant returns to capital, and it is assumed that capital is the only determinant of long-run economic growth of output. Jones used empirical data of 15 OECD countries over the period of 1950–1988 and found no evidence supporting the prediction of the AK model. His time series tests include advanced econometric tests known as Dickey–Fuller tests. These tests show that rates of investment especially for equipment have risen persistently over time, while GDP growth rates have not. For more recent periods of 1950–2004 and for a larger number of countries, the advanced time series tests are reported in Sengupta (2010). This confirms the Jones hypothesis. Only exceptions are two countries: China and Taiwan.

The second hypothesis of the endogenous growth theory is also rejected by the OECD sample used by Jones. In rejecting the endogenous growth models Jones suggested an alternative that he calls "semiendogenous" growth. In this formulation growth occurs due to the development of new intermediate inputs (or outputs) by forward-looking firms as in the models of Romer (1990). It is assumed that the R&D costs of creating new intermediate inputs are inversely proportional to the number of existing inputs. Recently Feenstra et al. (1997) have tested this semiendogenous growth model by using sectional data for South Korea and Taiwan. They tested the relationship between changes in product variety and the growth in TFP across Taiwan and Korea in 16 sectors over 1975–1991. Their empirical estimates lend support to the prediction of the semiendogenous growth models. They find that changes in relative product variety viewed as either a lag or a lead have positive and significant effect on TFP in 8 of the 16 sectors. Seven out of these eight sectors rely on technology-intensive manufactured inputs and seem to fit the idea of endogenous growth. Among the primary industries that rely more heavily on natural resources or low level of technology, they found mixed to little evidence. Taiwan has a higher level of product variety than Korea in a number of secondary industries as follows.

	Level of product variety in Taiwan relative to Korea	TFP (%)	
		Korea	Taiwan
Food products	37.3	2.55	3.01
Chemicals	25.3	1.52	1.10
Machinery	15.3	2.79	−0.59
Instruments	7.8	4.13	0.72

Thus, the economic results based on regressions indicate that the primary industries do not support the prediction of the semiendogenous growth model, but the secondary industry results provide quite strong support. The division of industries into two groups, namely, primary and secondary, was intended to capture the degree to which industries relied on technology-intensive differentiated manufacturing inputs.

We may now present some stylized facts about the growth episodes in these countries.

For Taiwan the most dynamic element in its rapid economic growth is its IT sector and the growth in information industry. From 1995 to 1999 its information industry ranked third in the world after the USA and Japan. The state's strong leadership in R&D and related investment in the IT sector started in 1982, when the value of exports of IT products was only $106 million in US dollars. But by 1985 these exports climbed to $1.22 billion representing about 3.9% of all exports. In 1992 the computer products accounted for 42% of the country's exports. The overall R&D intensity rose from 1.78 in 1995 to 2.16 in 2003 and has exceeded 2.90 in 2008. The World Economic Forum Report has computed a growth competitive index (GCI) based on three components: infrastructure development, quality of public institutions, and the adoption of best practice technology of the world. Its report for 2002–2004 showed the following ranking among selected countries.

	Rank (2002)	Rank (2003)	Technology rank (2003)
Taiwan	6	5	3
Korea	25	18	6
Finland	1	1	2
Japan	16	11	5
USA	2	2	1
India	54	53	64
China	38	42	65

Clearly for a small country like Taiwan, this record of performance is most impressive. We may also note that in terms of the average number of annual US patents per million people, the top rankings in the world in 2004 were: USA (1), Japan (2), and Taiwan (3).

The second key element in Taiwan's economic growth is technical efficiency gain. This refers to the productivity effectiveness of a country's endowments: human and physical capital, other resources such as knowledge capital, etc. Some estimates by the World Bank of technical efficiency change over the period of 1960–1989 are as follows.

Latin America	−1.421
Sub-Saharan Africa	−3.453
Hong Kong	1.971
Japan	0.988
Taiwan	0.843
South Korea	−0.204

Over the period of 1995–2000 the Taiwan economy underwent transition from the traditional to the modern technology system. From 1970 onward Taiwan made special efforts to promote high-tech exports through publicly funded research efforts and improved education policies. New economic reforms initiated in 1990 put extra emphasis on technology and skill-intensive activities, e.g., IT, electronics, and telecommunications equipment. The following estimates reveal the economic picture very clearly.

	1995	2000
Export/GDP (%)	42.03	47.66
Gross investment/GDP (%)	24.93	22.57
Export growth rate (%)	20.0	21.98
Secondary-school enrollment rate (%)	95.93	99.61
Higher-education enrollment rate (%)	45.32	60.85
Output of the IT sector Total (US $ billions)	15.4 (1990)	69.8 (2005)
Information products	6.9 (1990)	35.0 (2005)
Consumer electronics	2.3 (1990)	7.0 (2005)

The above data are from Hobday (1995) updated for recent years. What is unique about this growth feature is that this has consistently improved over more recent years from 2006 to 2010. We have to note that the Taiwan Council for Economic Planning and Development prepared a 10-year plan (1980–1989) that provided targets for R&D expenditures and human capital supply. The targets have been mostly fulfilled as Taiwan followed world leaders in high-tech fields in the IT and telecommunications sector.

Another unique feature of this growth episode is the high degree of technology diffusion across medium- and small-sized enterprises. Without sacrificing technical efficiency this diffusion has utilized the spillover effects and efficiency in a decentralization fashion, resulting in growth with more equitable distribution. Taiwan provides the classic example where the Kuznets hypothesis of rising inequality with economic growth fails to hold. The Gini coefficients for land and income estimated by Rodrick (1994) portray this pattern as follows.

	Land	Income
Korea	0.39	0.34
Taiwan	0.46	0.31
India	0.52	0.42
Mexico	0.69	0.53
Japan	0.47	0.40

Clearly the NICs in Asia exhibit more equalitarian distribution of income along with rapid growth episodes.

Korea's growth episode resembles the pattern of other successful NICs in Asia. Recent annual growth rate of income per capita has exceeded 7.6% over 1985–1995 accompanied by high investment rate exceeding 7.1%. High capital formation has been financed to a large extent by high natural savings. Productivity and efficiency gains have provided the key sources of growth. The trade regime has favored export expansion. World competition has been a powerful force for enforcing domestic competition. The private sector has been a powerful engine of growth in both domestic and foreign trade. South Korea's export boom amounted to about 35% of GDP during the 1990s, and most of it was in the nontraditional goods such as color TV and electronic goods. The record of export performance in IT products and technical services has been very significant. The share of IT products and services in total merchandise exports through 1980–1989 has grown from 10 in 1980 to 22 in 1989 and rose much higher in 2000. In Japan it rose from 14 in 1980 to 28 in 1989, while for Taiwan the comparable figures are 14 and 25.

The IT sector has played a significant role in accelerating the growth of exports. This sector has also helped in the process of technology diffusion. The rates of growth of output per worker in Korea have been 5.3 and 5.2 in 1973–1984 and 1984–1994, and both physical capital and the education level have made significant contributions. The role of IT investment in Korean economic growth is as follows.

	1981–1985		1996–2000	
	Av. annual growth rate (%)	Contribution	Av. annual growth rate (%)	Contribution
GDP	7.5	100	4.7	100
IT capital	0.2	3	0.4	8
Labor	1.07	14	0.37	8
TFP	4.36	55	9.39	74
IT contribution	0.66	8	8.4	66

These estimates are from Kim (2002) who used production function methods to estimate TFP and the contribution of IT capital. His analysis showed that the IT sector investment has helped diffuse productivity in other sectors of the Korean economy.

The key to long-term sustainable growth in India in the recent phase from 2008 onward lies in the contribution of knowledge capital to overall output growth. The best proxy for this knowledge capital is R&D investment, which improves domestic innovation and provides important linkages for technology transfer from the USA. Some estimates of overall cost elasticity with respect to R&D knowledge capital reported by Sengupta (2005) is found to be positive and lower than unity during 1995–2004. This implies that the Korean economy is in a better position today to absorb and spread new innovations and that the private sector plays a more dominant role here. This trend would intensify in the coming years as technology competition increases.

6.4 Learning by Doing and Efficiency Growth

For the last three decades the industrial economies have undergone some dramatic changes. Technology, innovation, and information networks have expanded worldwide. Markets have become worldwide; knowledge in information technology has spread far and wide as the computer industry revolution has occurred. Two major dynamic changes have their dramatic impact, which is certainly growing more and more in effect. One is the dynamic shift from large-scale manufacturing to the design and use of new ICT. This new technology diffusion is associated with a significant degree of increasing returns to scale and what is sometimes called a positive feedback effect. This has also generated large spillover effects, which induce new technology knowledge transfer from the industrial to the developing countries. The most successful NICs in Asia have utilized this dynamic shift to their comparative advantage.

A second dynamic change is that the efficiency concept has been expanded considerably since the Schumpeterian framework of innovation. The new efficiency concepts include, besides the standard production efficiency, some of the following mechanisms: (1) access efficiency, (2) innovation efficiency, (3) resource efficiency, and (4) adaptive efficiency. These concepts are discussed later.

In recent times competition has been most intense in high-tech industries such as computers, microelectronics, and semiconductors. Product and process innovations, economies of scale, and learning by doing have intensified the competitive pressure, leading to declining prices and unit costs due to high productivity growth. For example average computer prices declined by 18% per year from 1960 to 1995 and by 27% per year over 1995–1998. Recent estimates for 1998–2004 exceed 28% per year. For the NICs the collaboration with foreign direct investment and improving the imported technical knowledge borrowed from abroad have helped their R&D investments and learning economies to grow. They were, thus, able to compete very successfully in the world market for technology-intensive products.

Also they utilized the various types of dynamic efficiency mentioned before. These efficiencies have different features, e.g., production efficiency is competing in the price and quantity area. The NICs have proved most successful in world competition today. Then there is access efficiency, which consists of competing in the strongholds arena. Goods made by one company or one country become available anywhere in the world. Thus, market expansion facilitates the exploitation of increasing returns to scale and the spillover effects. Then there is resource efficiency where competition begins in the deep-pocketed arena. Companies and countries expand their resource base and use their assets to build their next temporary advantage before other competitors move in. China used this strategy to move into new arenas of world competition. China's technological improvement has benefited significantly from the country's imports of foreign capital and technology, as well as increasing investment in education and R&D. Both the state and the private sector have been very active in human capital and knowledge creation. For example in 2003 about 34% of education expenditure and 76% of total R&D spending came from private nongovernment sources. Even then China's share of spending on education and R&D in total GDP is well below than those in the world's major economies. For example most OECD countries spend thrice as much as China does on R&D. However, the state policy in China is trying very hard to augment the investment in R&D and education. This policy has adopted different strategies such as the development of a venture capital market, establishment of science and technology markets, introduction of R&D bonds and incentives for the promotion of domestic R&D activities. China has some way to go on the innovation efficiency front. For example about half of the patent filings in China in 2004 were made by foreign companies in China, while most in Japan and South Korea were by local investors. This suggests that China still has to try to develop home-grown technology before it participates fully in the world scientific and innovation league.

Most NICs in Asia have taken the innovation efficiency challenge very seriously. For example the Long-Term Plan for Development of Science and Technology (2006–2020) has been introduced by the Chinese government in 2006 to turn China into an "innovation oriented society" by the year 2020. This plan commits China's development of capabilities for indigenous innovation. Other Asian countries such as Malaysia have started adopting more innovative policies for improving their technological performance in high-tech exports in global trade. India is not lagging behind; its IT sector is improving at a fast rate.

Chapter 7
Evolutionary Economics

Economic growth viewed as evolution of economic systems is a new paradigm developed in the last two decades. This paradigm is a challenge to the neoclassical models of growth. It has three major facets. The first is the emphasis on dynamic capability and core competence as the basic forces of economic change. The second is the Schumpeterian model of "innovations" where the "entrepreneur" plays an active role in creating new combinations in the production and marketing process. The third is the economic application of the generic theory of evolution, where the principle of survival of the fittest is applied to explain industry growth.

The neoclassical models of growth emphasize essentially the role of the competitive market. Recent developments in information technology and global trade have significantly changed the market structure and the investment pattern. They have also challenged the world of competitive equilibria and their guiding principles. For the last two decades the advances in industrial economies have undergone some dramatic changes. Technology, innovations, and information flows have expanded worldwide. Markets have expanded, information and communications technology have spread, and knowledge diffusion has occurred through the growth of the computer industry. All these have caused a dynamic shift away from large-scale manufacturing to the design and use of new information technology. This new technology is characterized by positive feedback mechanisms, which generate increasing returns to scale and externalities in the form of spillover effects. As a result, noncompetitive market structures have developed, and institutions other than markets have played active roles in initiating new economic changes and growth. Non-Walrasian adjustment mechanisms and game-theoretic models have been increasingly invoked to explain the recent economic evolution in terms of dynamic capability and adaptive efficiency. The traditional Schumpeterian model of innovation has found significant extensions in recent times. Structural transformations of the economy and the role of dynamic efficiency and productivity have been increasingly invoked. This aspect is closely related to the Darwinian principle of survival of the fittest. Evolutionary stable strategies of the evolutionary game model have found their application in the recent application of evolutionary economics to explain the successful growth of new industries.

J. Sengupta, *Understanding Economic Growth: Modern Theory and Experience*,
DOI 10.1007/978-1-4419-8026-7_7, © Springer Science+Business Media, LLC 2011

7.1 Dynamic Capability and Adaptive Efficiency

Dynamic capability models have emphasized specific strategies for economic change, which foster firm and industry growth. Winter (2008) has recently discussed examples of some of these strategies. Escalating the miniaturization trajectory for the personal computers and communication equipment is one example. Innovations for iPad by Apple, etc., are another example. Replication is another growth strategy, e.g., dynamic capabilities here create new units as in the franchise system of McDonald corporation, by which a large number of smaller operating units extends the geographic scope and widens the markets.

A second aspect of dynamic capability deals with the strategy of adaptivity of human capital. As Nelson and Phelps (1966) showed that adaptive human capital not only facilitates the adoption of more advanced technology but also makes it easier to innovate at the technology frontier. The economic ecologists suggest that there are several internal and external barriers to the ability of organizations to achieve adaptive efficiency as follows: (1) the path dependence of firms as organizations, i.e., their own history which tends to keep status quo, (2) specialized personnel and specialized production network, (3) large switching costs to technology transfer, and (4) high degree of risk aversion by the executives due to incomplete markets, where there exists only limited facilities for optimal trade in risky resources.

The emergence of Silicon Valley and rapid growth of the computer technology for the last 15 years have created a whole set of new markets. These markets are new institutions that create new types of firms and organizations that are flatter, more networked, and more flexible. Thus, they are much quicker to take advantage of any new opportunities. The new firms adopt a faster strategy to learn and change constantly due to the pressure of fierce hypercompetition. Adaptive efficiency plays a key role in the new institutional structure. It intensifies the process of learning by doing and the development of tacit knowledge that will lead the executives to increase economic efficiency. Adaptive efficiency provides the incentives to encourage the development of decentralized decision making, which imparts more flexibility in initiating new changes and product developments.

There exist three basic forces for firms as institutions to initiate and adopt new changes in strategies. The first is the presence of increasing returns associated with the information technology. The second is the persistence of imperfect markets for institutions and organizations due to the existence of significant transaction costs. Coase and North have developed growth models for institutions, where growth and efficiency are significantly impaired due to the presence of large transactions costs. The presence of large increasing returns due to a significant degree of fixed cost already sunk in the status quo puts up a strong barrier to change and the adoption of a new institutional structure and new technology. The third force shaping the path of institutional growth is to adopt a R&D investment strategy that is fast, innovative, and risk taking under the given information structure. For this purpose the firm should be organized as multidimensional or M-form where the CEO is at the top with a functional decentralization into manufacturing, sales, distribution, finance, and R&D divisions.

According to Williamson (1985) it is the most significant organizational innovation of the twentieth century. The essential feature of the M-form is that the profit responsibility is decentralized to the level of individual product lines, individual brands, and individual geographic markets. As examples of success of this organizational form and all progressive forms, we may refer to three case histories. The first is the Pilkington Glass which spent more than 7 years and 21 million dollars to perfect its new float plate glass process. This innovation sustained Pilkington's dominance in the glass industry. The second case refers to Sony's strategy in sticking to beta VCR system and thereby losing the market. The need for understanding the future trends in technology is more adequately assessed in the progressive organizations. The third example is that of China and its rapid growth episode, where foreign competition and large-scale FDI provided a powerful force to combat bureaucracy and inertia in Chinese economic systems. Three aspects of China's measures of economic reform are to be noted here. First, the state sector had to start a steady shift away from bureaucratic control towards profitability and a decentralized managerial system. Second, the policy of voluntary mergers for state enterprises was adopted in the 1990s in order to enhance efficiency. This helped to reduce transactions costs and to augment the utilization of increasing returns. Finally, China emphasized in its long-term goal to adopt the endogenous innovation as the target for the next decade. Strategies adopted so far are both proactive in that new markets and new opportunities are being explored by diverting Chinese investment abroad and also reactive in that China has taken steps to correct its competition disadvantage through more openness in trade. The membership of WTO has indicated China's strong commitment in this regard.

Dynamic capability has been emphasized as "core competence" by managerial discipline. Prahalad and Hamel (1990) defines it as "the collective learning in the organization," especially how to coordinate diverse production skills and integrate multiple streams of technologies. Three basic components of core competence are: learning, coordinating, and integrating. Learning by doing has been the key strategy in the high growth miracles of the NICs in Asia. The examples of China and Taiwan are noteworthy. China's entry into WTO by the end of 2001 has intensified the new economic reform process introduced in the 1990s. The rapid increase in China's openness in international trade resulted in the rapid increase in China's share of world exports. The exports share in some products such as wearing apparel, electronics, and business and finance rose from 19.58, 1.92 and 1.91% in 1995 to 45.14, 2.58, and 2.59% in 2005, respectively. The growth of FDI over the recent period of 2000–2009 has been phenomenal. Learning by doing spread very far and wide in China due to its close trade relation with Taiwan. Taiwan is most successful in the coordinating and integrating aspects of core competence.

Coordination failure has posed a serious economic obstacle for many less-developed economies. Large investments have failed due to lack of coordination. This is especially true for state-sponsored projects. Coordination failure has posed enormous problems in many underdeveloped economies in their development projects.

Coordination is crucial to the IT task. Recent trends in off shoring of IT and related technology to India, China, and other countries are largely due to the fact that many newer tasks of IT jobs do not need close coordination. Thus, one reason IT jobs have remained in the USA despite low wages in India is that the US programmers are advantaged at completing tasks where coordination with other UD based workers is also needed in finding the best use of resources, but the pattern of best use is always changing due to the new technology. Organization flexibility and adaption is, thus, crucial for success. NICs in Asia such as Taiwan and Singapore always emphasized this aspect of adaptive efficiency and dynamic capability. Coordination and control also affect agency costs because structures designed for similar tasks may differ in the opportunities they offer managers to pursue personal or unit objectives that are inconsistent with the firm's objectives. Transaction costs increase when coordination failure occurs, and as a result economic inefficiency develops.

Taiwan also provides the case of a successful provider of the integration function of core competence. Its R&D work resulting in record patents in the world is one clear evidence, since research activity in the high-tech field today is highly integrative. It needs fine team work and persistent learning by doing. Its successful decentralization of high-tech processes to medium and small enterprises also bears testimony to this competence. Countries such as India and Malaysia need to work hard to succeed in this arena. One has to note that the competence perspective and evolutionary approach of Nelson and Winter (1982) both have fundamentally an efficiency approach to firm performance. The modern evolutionary economists emphasize the role of many types and dimensions of innovations. Some innovations may be competence-destroying, others competence-enhancing. As Schumpeter emphasized that in the dynamic case of today's high-tech world the path dependence of the technology frontier of the firm and the industry may render the old technology paradigm obsolete and destroy the firm's basis of competition by introducing new resource requirements. Creative destruction, however, initiates the need for new creative accumulation of knowledge capital and core competence.

7.2 Schumpeterian Innovation Model

Schumpeter's approach to innovation and industry growth is dynamic and broad based. It has three key components. First, it views the central problem of evolutionary economics: dynamics of growth. He challenges the equilibrium and optimization paradigms of the neoclassical model. Competition is basically dynamic, and the dynamic entrepreneurs innovate for profits and therefore attempt to destroy old equilibria by establishing new combinations. If successful, these entrepreneurs enjoy significant profits, and their regime continues till they are displaced by new innovations. Second, he proposed a model of creative destruction, where new productivity gains drive economic growth. In addition, dynamic competition forced by innovation flows provides the necessary transfer of productivity gains to consumers in the form of lower prices, resulting in an increase in fiscal welfare through gains in consumer surplus. Finally, his contribution develops a model of industry growth through his emphasis on the following aspects:

1. Innovation depends heavily on the capacity of firms to invest in R&D activities. Large firms have the resource efficiency to build more capacity to innovate.
2. The gains from innovation are largely internalized by the dynamic entrepreneurs.
3. Increased profits by the successful innovations help to augment the innovation flow better.
4. Schumpeter's concept of innovation is viewed as the setting up of a new production function by creating new combinations of outputs, inputs, or their transformations.

Economic evolution of industry is characterized by an upward-moving neighborhood of equilibrium with two phases. One phase moves the production network from one level of equilibrium, and the other is to follow the trajectory of the new equilibrium. According to Schumpeter the essence of capitalistic growth is the introduction of new combinations.

Schumpeter's concept of dynamic competition is essentially based on the concepts of dynamic efficiency through flexibility in a hypercompetitive framework we discussed before. Unlike the neoclassical theory this dynamic competition is an evolutionary process model, i.e., it is the disequilibriating evolutionary process that consists of constant struggle between firms for comparative advantage over time in the industrial markets. This is an endogenous growth process where there exist three important forces causing economic evolution. The first is the dynamic role of profits. It is not savings but profits from investment in innovation that lead to further innovations, which lead to sustained growth of the industry and hence the economy. Second, the endogenous process called "creative destruction" revolutionizes the economic structure of industry development from within. The large monopolistic firms bring new innovations into effect in their hunt for supernormal profits. Finally, the flexibility in bringing about innovations provides the third force causing economic evolution. This flexibility has two aspects: one for bringing about particular innovations and the other for setting up ongoing production processes to facilitate dealing with new situations.

Schumpeter's model of creative destruction may be approached in two ways. One is the creative aspect, and the other is the diffusion aspect. Creative accumulation of knowledge capital and creative ventures involve substantial R&D investment, which involves significant risks but the profit expectations are also very high. High profit incentives keep firms searching for ways to explore opportunities through imitation of new technology and piecemeal innovative activities. Schumpeterian notion of technological change is that creative entrepreneurs, e.g., Microsoft and Apple CEOs, see and implement new "business combinations" and force creative destruction on old and inefficient activities through dynamic monopolistic competition. Eliasson (1988) has discussed this from the viewpoint of scale economies associated with creative destruction. These scale economies occur through Adam

Smith's division of labor and also the externality effects, which influence microbehavior. The microbehavior spreads the process of technology diffusion on to the macrobehavior.

Schumpeter laid great stress on the dynamic entrepreneur who has the right foresight to take risks and introduce creative innovations. He performs a more dynamic role than the auctioneer in the Walrasian neoclassical model. The auctioneer is a heuristic fiction, while Schumpeterian entrepreneur is a real agent who responds to disequilibrium by arbitrage. The auctioneer is attempting to establish a long-run equilibrium, but Schumpeter's entrepreneur attempts to disrupt existing temporary equilibria to earn quasi-monopoly profits.

Schumpeter's concept of innovation is the modern concept of process innovations involving technical change embodied in physical capital. Heertje (1988) has recently used some characteristics of Schumpeter's innovation in the setting up of a new production function. First, the theoretical production function can be viewed as subjective or objective types. The subjective variant comprises the technical possibilities known to the firm. This production function does not reflect the general state of technology. The objective variant reflects technology in general. As a rule, new empirical production functions are brought about by innovations and new theoretical production functions by inventions. Second, the diffusion process transfers subject knowledge within a firm into general information about the new methods of production and new products. According to Schumpeter innovations are taken very broadly so that commercial and organizational changes and even the exploration of new markets are also implied. Finally, the evolutionary theory of economic growth developed by Nelson and Winter (1982), which centers on nonmaximizing firms, has much in common with Schumpeter's thinking.

Recent upsurges in knowledge capital and information technology have surpassed the Schumpeterian innovation concept in two directions. One is the rapid development of high-tech industries with significant increasing returns to scale and it has helped expand the global market. The rapid growth of NICs in Asia provides a classical example of this dynamic process. In the other direction, the market structure has become more and more hypercompetitive. As D'Aveni (1994) argues in his analysis of hypercompetitive strategies that in industries ranging from consumer electronics to computer software, the sources of dynamic competitive advantages are being created and eroded at an increasingly rapid rate. Hence, for success, a firm's chief strategic goal should be to disrupt existing sources of advantage in its industry and create new ones. This creates an innovation race to win and succeed.

7.3 Models of Industry Growth

Schumpeter's innovation approach to evolutionary economics contains the basic elements of a dynamic model of industry growth. It is useful, therefore, to analyze the industry dynamics where innovations play a crucial role. Sengupta (2007) has discussed in some detail the models of industry evolution, which incorporate the flow of innovation investment. These models are based on the following relationships, which contain the basic ingredients of the Schumpeterian theory:

1. The rate of growth of innovations depends on two factors: the gap of the advanced technology from the existing one and the knowledge capital. Schumpeter stressed mostly on the first aspect.
2. Unit cost declines due to investment in innovations. This results in excess profits for the leading firms who adopt advanced technology.
3. Profits from investment lead to further innovations. Diffusion of knowledge capital and externalities provide incentives for other firms and industries to innovate and invest.
4. Birth rate of new innovations and R&D provides the positive side of industry evolution, while the death rate provides the negative side. The contagion effect of birth rates influences other firms to invest in R&D.
5. Long-term profit maximization and faster rates of growth provide the basic incentives for firms to innovate. The industry evolution and hence the overall growth of the industrial economy are in essence driven by productivity and efficiency growth.

The relations above can be used to develop a dynamic model of industry growth, where the trajectories would indicate the paths of endogenous evolution. Scale economies and profit incentives are the two key forces in this growth paradigm. Innovation in both physical and knowledge capital is the driving force of this hyper-competitive market structure and does not reflect the mere numbers of agents in the supply side of markets. Innovations depend heavily on the capacity of firms to invest in R&D activities. This investment is strongly correlated with the sizes and market shares of firms. The large firms tend to have comparative advantages due to its large resource basis and accumulated supply of creative knowledge applicable to industrial fields.

7.4 Evolutionary Economics

The theory of evolutionary economics interprets industry and economic growth as evolution of economic systems in an open economy. It has three key strands. First, it borrows from the genetic evolution theory the concepts of survival of the fittest and applies it to explain the process of growth of firms and industries. Second, it refers to organizational efficiency and structural characteristics of technology and the institutional framework of an economy and their dynamic capabilities. Finally, it is clearly related to the theory of evolutionary stable strategies in recent genetic theory whereby one species gain competitive advantage over others and sustain their reproductive efficiency. The successful firms adopt these strategies in competition for R&D race and innovations. We discuss here these three strands of evolutionary economics, which explain the process of industry growth and therefore the overall economic growth.

Evolutionary economists have borrowed the Fisherian concept of genetic evolution of species for the analysis of industry growth. Some aspects of this theory are relevant here. First, it is based on the fitness principle, which is closely related to the Darwinian model in natural selection of species. In market competition the leading firms, which are innovation-efficient, develop technological edge and acquire a dominant share of the market. Owing to significant cost and quality advantage they gain new entry and displace the old incumbent. In genetic models "entry" is comparable to invasion of one species by another. Fitness of species is comparable to dynamic efficiency of firms. Second, the dynamic fitness principle is comparable to the management science concept of *core competence* as the source of industry growth. Finally, the concept of evolutionary competition borrowed from the genetic theory has been applied by Metcalfe (1994) and Dosi (1984) and others to model the dynamic evolution of new technologies. The key point in their approach is that the rate of change in unit costs due to the emergence of new technology is proportional to the weighted variance of unit costs in the industry. This implies that as technology spreads and the variance of unit costs rises, the mature technologies would show a slower rate of growth than the new technologies. But as dynamic competition proceeds, the surviving firms and technologies have not only a higher average productivity but a lower productivity variance too. But this may lead to a switch to a new technology paradigm, as new streams of technology follow.

The fitness principle underlying Fisher's fundamental theorem of natural selection in unlimited environments has dominated the thinking of population biologists for a long time. Fisher's theorem states that the average fitness of the population of a species never decreases in the course of natural selection in unlimited environments. Recently adaptivity in the selection process has been introduced in population dynamics in two ways. One is to postulate that the rate of change in the growth rate of a species is a function of the environment. The other is to apply the evolutionary stable strategies proposed by Smith (1982), where the species following these strategies succeed in the long run. The fitness principle with adaptivity in the environment has been applied to the dynamics of market competition by Metcalfe (1994), Dosi (1984), and Nelson and Winter (1982). Here average unit costs are a proxy for fitness, where average fitness depends critically on the new technology and innovation flow in the industry. Thus, firms with more efficient technology tend to lead the industry growth. The dynamics of Schumpeterian competition changes technology at various points of the value chain. Both incremental and nonincremental innovations create disruptive dynamics and transform the technologies.

Organizational efficiency through learning by doing provides an important source of dynamics of industry growth. In Nelson and Winter's work the institutions and organizations played an active role because they focused on the persistent interaction between the institutional properties of the technological trajectory and the learning activities of firms. Recent evolution theorists have emphasized the theory of *interactive learning* as the main source of diffusion of knowledge. It involves both the introduction of knowledge and the diffusion of knowledge in the form of new products, services, or processes. Learning leads to new knowledge, and different kinds of entrepreneurs use this knowledge, e.g., new software to form innovative ideas and projects. Thus, diffusion through spillover effects and learning processes are inseparable, and they are mutually reinforcing. The patent system and the hypercompetitive market structure are the two key evolutionary selection mechanisms. Evolutionary economists recognize both the cumulative nature of technological change as well as the endogenous nature of market structures. Dynamic efficiency is their central principle of industry and market evolution.

Finally we consider a dynamic limit pricing model under innovations discussed in some detail by Sengupta and Fanchon (2009). Here one firm is dominant in view of its position as a leader in leading-edge technology, and the others are Bertrand-type followers in the competitive fringe. In this Bertrand–Nash equilibrium model the dominant firms may follow predatory pricing strategy in the short run so as to deter or eliminate the existing firms on the fringe. The success of this type of predator–prey strategy depends on the strategic behavior of the other players. This type of behavior underlies the well-known hawk–dove game example considered by Smith (1982). In this game the two species (hawk and dove) are competing for a common resource of value v, which increases the Darwinian fitness of a species. Thus, v is the gain in fitness to the winner, while c is the cost of an injury, which reduces fitness. The payoff matrix in terms of changes in fitness is as follows.

			$v=2$	$c=4$
	H	D	H	D
H	$(v-c)/2$	v	-1	2
D	0	$v/2$	0	1

Three assumptions behind the above payoff matrix of the symmetric game mentioned above are as follows: (1) hawk vs. hawk: each contestant has a 50% chance of injuring its opponent and obtaining the resource v and a 50% chance of being injured, (2) hawk vs. dove: hawk obtains the resource and dove retreats before being injured, and (3) dove vs. dove: the resource is shared equally by the two contestants.

Now consider an infinite population of individuals, each adopting the strategy H or D at random. In this model the higher fitness behavior has an advantage in reproducing. Thus, if the population consists of only doves, then this will continue in the next generation, but if there is a mutation that introduces a hawk in the population, then over time the fraction of doves in the population will decrease, and the fraction of hawks will increase. Similarly if the population consists entirely of hawks, a mutant dove can successfully invade the population. The only stable population is, thus, evenly divided between hawks and doves; here mutation would not disturb the population distribution. This is the idea of an evolutionary stable strategy (ESS), where the stable pattern of behavior in a population should be able to withstand any invasion by a mutant. Thus, if a population pattern of behavior is to withstand the invading mutations, it must have a higher fitness (i.e., higher payoff) than the mutant in the population.

The ESS strategies have two useful implications for evolutionary growth theory in economics. One is that it provides a more rational framework for the fitness model for the evolution of a leading-edge technology. The other is that the equilibrium distribution of products or processes under the framework of dynamic monopolistic competition may be viewed as a process analogous to the replicator dynamics. The replicator organizations pursue as a primary growth strategy the creation of an industrial world today. Most customer transactions in the USA today are becoming self-service digital transactions and intermediaries are evolving to add value or perish. Two implications of the Internet revolution are worth pointing out. In pre-Internet days the only way customers could get goods and services from manufacturers was through tiers of distribution and retailers. Today any manufacturer can provide the Internet equivalent of a factory outlet. Second most Web merchants, e.g., e-Bay or Amazon.com, offer flexible pricing, i.e., a policy to match the lowest price a consumer can find.

The globalization of demand and trade and the use of IT networks in communications imply that US growth of IT technology will have a significant diffusion effect. Here one may refer to the technological gap model of international competitiveness by Laursen (1999) who identified two important implications. The first implication is the structural market effect, i.e., the advantage coming from being initially specialized in goods that are export-sensitive. For example Taiwan, Hong Kong, and Singapore utilized this market effect to a significant degree. Second, there is a technology adaptation effect, i.e., the ability to move a larger number of substantially smaller operating units actively. The dynamic capabilities here are those of replication itself, i.e., capabilities that support the creation of new units, thereby extending the geographic scope of the activities of the replicator. Thus, the replicator organizations such as McDonald Corporation are particularly common in retail trade. Economies of scale and scope are their key sources of economic fitness. Thus, the successful firms in the high-tech field today have much to learn from the ESS strategies discussed in evolutionary game theory. The episode of success by the high-growth NICs in Asia, such as Taiwan and China, provides support to such evolutionary stable strategies in world competition.

7.5 Innovation Efficiency

Innovation efficiency is central to economic evolution and industry growth in this age of information technology and its rapid advance. Growth of human capital and R&D investments are likely to grow more and more over the coming years. This advance has gone much faster than Schumpeter visualized. The revolution of the information age is changing the face of the technological sectors with favorable rates of growth. Again the successful NICs in Asia have followed this strategy most persistently. Japan imitated the US technology and improved it significantly. As a result their market share of world exports of IT products has grown phenomenally over the years. Taiwan's record of new patents in IT products and processes is most remarkable. Antonelli (1995) estimated the regression function of average rate of growth of labor productivity on five variables, namely, GDP per capita, average investment to GDP ratio, total US patents, indicator of diffusion of IT technology (DIT), and a catching up variable for 25 representative industrial countries over the period of 1980–1988. His estimates found the DIT variable to be highly significant at 1% of *t*-test, and his overall results confirmed that the diffusion rates of key technologies in communications and information fields have generated significant knowledge spillover effects. The successful NICs in Asia have used these effects to innovate and grow. They borrowed, imitated, and learned. They coordinated and integrated. As a result they grew and improved their core competence.

Chapter 8
Growth

As a country develops, its income rises, and the industrial sector gains more importance than the agricultural sector. Industrial growth is the key to capitalistic development based on private markets. The general equilibrium paradigm and the competitive market mechanisms characterize this growth process. In recent times the growth of high-tech industries has challenged this paradigm. We would discuss here a few of these challenges as follows:

1. Information technology
2. Productivity
3. Growth and inequality
4. Market failure

The first two topics deal with the sources of economic growth and the last two with the structural impact of economic growth. These issues are important for the study of economic growth for two reasons. One is the structural reason, since it emphasizes the basic changes occurring in the world today. Productivity and economic efficiency are the ultimate determinants of growth in the modern world, and the competitive pressures of the global market have intensified the dynamic role of these twin sources. The other reason is concerned with the allocative process of the consequences of industry growth. Income inequality and the failure of competitive market mechanisms are two major problems before the capitalistic development process.

8.1 Information Technology

Traditionally technology is associated with the improvement in the use of technical processes in manufacturing and other forms of production. Thus, it may involve the improvement of productivity of the current and capital inputs, such as labor, physical capital, materials, and energy. Usually these inputs are rivalrous in the sense that they are not complementary, i.e., these compete with one another generating diminishing returns to scale. After a certain level of output each of these inputs yields diminishing marginal products. Modern technology is different

J. Sengupta, *Understanding Economic Growth: Modern Theory and Experience*,
DOI 10.1007/978-1-4419-8026-7_8, © Springer Science+Business Media, LLC 2011

in outlook. It involves improvement in the productivity of knowledge and R&D investment viewed as "knowledge capital." Modern industries in the developed countries are increasingly characterized by this new type of technology based on knowledge capital. The growth miracles experienced by the NICs in Asia in the last two decades all evidenced remarkable productivity gains through the fast accumulation of knowledge capital. This type of capital is complementary to all other inputs traditionally associated with the concept of a production function. Thus, it is nonrivalrous and noncompetitive. It yields constant or increasing returns (IR) to scale, and its marginal product does not diminish. Furthermore, it has externality or spillover effects through the process of learning by doing and creative diffusion. Its scale effects tend to support wider markets through lower unit costs and prices, and hence, globalization of markets helps other countries and other industries through dynamic gains of international trade. Foreign direct investment and transnational business have expanded the markets through the transfer of his new technology. An economy characterized by this new technology is often called "the new knowledge economy," and it has four fundamental characteristics: accumulating knowledge capital, improving competitive efficiency, expanding export markets through global trade, and increasing collaboration and mergers in the creation and diffusion of new knowledge capital, which has significant spillover effects. Knowledge capital may take several forms, e.g., (a) software development, (b) new designs and blueprints, (c) R&D activity, and (d) skill in the use of human capital such as learning. Competitive efficiency refers to using market process by which entrepreneurs trade in technology license and knowledge to improve their profitability. Openness in trade through exports and imports involves competition and mergers to improve overall economic efficiency. The strategies of MNCs to internalize some of the spillover effects of R&D benefits have led to collaborative arrangement with domestic entrepreneurs, and the governments of many successful NICs in Asia such as Taiwan, China, and South Korea have exploited this collaborative arrangement to develop very successfully their own ventures. The increasing number of R&D patents in New York granted to Taiwan competes very successfully with the number of US patents today.

8.2 Productivity

In global markets today competitive efficiency holds the key to success. Several important aspects of this efficiency have to be noted. The most important aspect of competitiveness is national productivity and specially the productivity of those sectors using information technology and software services. Porter (1990) investigated for 4 years why nations gain competitive advantage, studying ten important countries, Denmark, Germany, Italy, Japan, South Korea, Singapore, Sweden, Switzerland, the UK, and the USA, and reached three important conclusions. First, sustained productivity growth at the industry level requires that an economy continually upgrades itself. An upgrading economy is one that develops the capability of competitive success in entirely new and sophisticated industries. Doing so absorbs human resources released in the process of improving productivity in existing fields. The second aspect of competitive advantage is to compete in international trade through eliminating the need to produce all goods and services within the country itself and therefore specializing in goods and services where it is most cost-efficient. Finally, one must note that governments cannot create competitive industries, only private firms and industries can. The best example is provided by Japan, which is currently being followed by Taiwan, South Korea, Singapore, and China. The Japanese government encourages developing cooperative policies for adopting frontier up-to-date technologies and speeds up the process of upgrading and improving innovations.

Recently international competitive businesses have undergone a transformation from large-scale material manufacturing to the design and use of new technologies intensive in software use and application. This has generated a shift from diminishing returns to IR process. These IR-based technologies have been very successfully adopted and followed by the most successful NICs in Asia, which have achieved high growth rates for over two decades. Maintaining sustained dynamic efficiency has been central to their growth policy. This dynamic efficiency has four aspects: production efficiency, innovation efficiency, access efficiency, and resource efficiency. We may discuss these aspects briefly. Racing up the ladder in the cost and quality arena creates production efficiency. This is the central emphasis of the Walrasian model of competition equilibria. Second, racing up the escalation ladder in the know-how and learning-by-doing arena creates innovation efficiency.

Competing in the strongholds arena leads to access efficiency. Goods and services produced by one company become available worldwide so that customers everywhere have access to a wider variety of goods and services. This generates economies of scale in demand. Finally, there is resource efficiency, where the companies race up the escalation ladder in the deep-pockets arena. The creation of new strategic assets by the efficient firms in the industry through R&D efforts is very often used by the successful innovator. The story of IBM is often cited here. IBM bet the company for the 360 series computers, and the bet paid off in the 1960s. But its resources were unable to sustain its position in the next temporary advantage phase, i.e., the PC market. Instead tiny companies such as Apple and Microsoft become giants by seizing the next advantage. The challenge before them now is to invest their newly found deep pockets to build the next temporary advantage phase.

Efficiency-driven growth in the knowledge capital-intensive industries today has replaced the paradigm of productivity gains discussed by Porter. It has always changed the market structure in a drastic manner. The new economic environment favors increased concentration by the dominant firms, and the MNCs have a significant role to play.

We may also point out the role of economic and political institutions in the economic environment, where we emphasize organizational efficiency and managerial competence. Core competence has been defined as the collective learning in the organization, especially in learning how to coordinate diverse production skills and integrate multiple streams of technologies. Four basic elements of core competence are as follows: learn, coordinate, integrate, and innovate. Countries such as Taiwan and Singapore have adopted this strategy and achieved very high growth rates. China and India are trying to follow this path along with other NICs in Asia.

Another concept of efficiency which is important for economic growth is "adaptive efficiency." We do not know all the aspects of adaptive efficiency, but clearly the overall institutional structure plays a key role. That economy which encourages the trials, experiments, and innovations we can characterize as adaptively efficient. The incentives embedded in the institutional framework motivate the process of learning by doing and adopt the desired systems of economic structure. Adaptive efficiency provides the mechanism to encourage the development of decentralized decision making that allows societies to maximize their efforts required to explore alternative ways of solving inefficiency problems. Institutional change and reforms offer important strategies here. Two forces shape institutional change. One is IR and the other is imperfect markets characterized by significant transactions costs. In a world where there are no IR and markets are perfectly competitive, institutions do not matter. Efficiency paradigm is sustained in this Walrasian competitive equilibrium.

8.3 Inequality

Kuznets (1955) examined the historical relationship between income per capita and income distribution. His analysis based on international cross-section data suggested that at low income levels economic growth and average income tended to create more income inequality as measured by the Gini coefficient. The Gini coefficient is expressed geometrically by the Lorenz curve that draws cumulative percentage distribution of household incomes in the vertical axis corresponding to cumulative distributions of the number of households in the horizontal axis ranked according to household incomes from the bottom to the top. Higher values of Gini coefficient denote higher inequality. Kuznets found in his empirical investigation that as per capita income continues to increase, a critical threshold level of income is reached and further economic growth and even higher average income tended to reduce income inequality. This is usually referred to as the Kuznets inverted-U hypothesis, from the shape of the curve generated.

So far it has been difficult to statistically confirm the inverted-U shape pattern from the time series data. Hayami and Gogo (2005) fitted a quadratic regression equation to explain the Gini coefficient in terms of several explanatory variables such as GDP per capita and country-specific dummy variables. Their data included 45 countries in various years within the period 1900–2000 in relation with their 1990–2000 average GDP per capita. The estimates are as follows:

$$\text{Gini} = -29.0 + 12.3\ln(Y/N) - 0.91\ln(Y/N)^2 - 12.3D(\text{CP}) + 12.1D(A) + 13.3D(L),$$

$$R^2 = 0.677.$$

Here Y/N is per capita GDP, $D(\mathrm{CP})$, $D(A)$, and $D(L)$ are three dummy variables for the centrally planned economies, Africa and Latin America. Although this regression supports the Kuznets hypothesis (i.e., positive coefficient for the quadratic term), the estimated coefficients are not statistically significant at 5% level. The dummy variables for Africa and Latin America are statistically significant at 1% level, suggesting that the country-specific inequality is more amenable to statistical explanation.

We have to note, however, that the Kuznets hypothesis suggests only a correlation pattern between rising income and inequality. The diversity of different countries and their structural differences do matter. Some stylized trends and tendencies have to be noted, however. First, Kuznets noted that the only country where inequality did not rise with income increase is Taiwan. Taiwan's average Gini coefficient for the period 1990–1995 is less than 13.0 for the whole economy, whereas for China it exceeds 23.7. For India (1994), Mexico (1996), Korea (1993), Brazil (1997), South Africa (1994), and China (1998), the coefficient values are 37.8, 51.9, 31.6, 59.1, 59.3, and 40.3, respectively. Two basic reasons for Taiwan's success in ensuring economic growth with equity may be cited. The first is its emphasis on widespread decentralization of the development process. Second, it emphasized the role of small and medium enterprises through state support much more vigorously than China and other NICs in Asia. A second point to note is that world income inequality is very high. In 1993 the poorest 10% of the world population had only 1.6% of the income of the richest 10%. Around 25% of the world population received in 2001 about 75% of the world income. And the richest 10% of the US population in 1993 (around 25 million people) had a combined income greater than that of the poorest 43% of the world population (around two billion people). This clearly suggests the need for large-scale development aid from the richest countries to the poorest ones. The World Bank and other international agencies have a more active role to play in this respect. A third aspect of income inequality associated with growth in the initial stages of development is to identify the sources and develop appropriate strategies as remedies. One important source is related to further shares. Assuming the two factors of labor and capital and their returns as wages and profits, the share of capital rises initially as investment increases. By using a Keynesian model with national income as the sum of wages and profits, it can be shown from the saving investment identity that the profit share of national income is a linear function of the investment share of income. Thus, the profit share rises as the investment share rises. If profit share can be used as a proxy for inequality of income distribution, then inequality would tend to rise as the investment rate rises. Note, however, that the Keynesian model uses a fixed coefficient production function and that it does not consider the elasticity of substitution between labor and capital. In the endogenous models of growth, however, the substitution between human and physical capital is directly admissible, and this may be an important reason for Taiwan's success in achieving more equality in income distribution. Another important reason for increasing inequality is the role of increasing monopoly elements due to the emergence of large and dominant firms in modern technology-intensive industries. The heavy investment by both the MNCs and FDI has intensified this process further. Since these investments have high fixed costs, they generate substantial scale economies. The scale economies act as deterrent to new entry of smaller and medium-size firms. Taiwan's economic policy prevented this from happening by encouraging the smaller and medium-size firms to have easy access to the technology-intensive fields. Also software technology and R&D activity requiring skilled human capital were strongly supported by the state policy. This helped maintain more equalitarian distribution of income.

8.4 Market Failure

The dynamics of industry growth, technology, and globalization have a dramatic impact on the current economic growth of nations today. They have challenged the Walrasian competition equilibrium model and their guiding principles. In the world of innovations and the spillover of R&D effects, various forms of noncompetitive market structures have evolved in recent times. This has sometimes been characterized as "market failures" associated with the deviations from the competitive market model. Four types of market failure would be discussed in this section as follows:

1. Externalities and spillover effects
2. Risk and uncertainty in financial markets
3. Transparency in information and technology markets
4. Market power and limit pricing

Externalities are the major source of deviations from the first-best optimum results in a competitive market. The externalities create two types of problems. One is the appropriability problem. If the R&D benefits for the single firm are not appropriable or internalizable, then the initial incentives to innovation and R&D investment are reduced. The other is that the cost reduction due to R&D investments that are largely fixed cost may lead to market concentration and imperfect competition with consequences for prices, profit margins, and allocative efficiency. Setting up entry barriers through predatory and limit pricing strategies may lead to substantial deviations from first-best optimal solution of a competitive market.

Spence (1984) has distinguished between anticipated and unanticipated spillovers. In the former case cooperative R&D might be useful. While cooperative R&D, which helps to internalize some of the externalities, is not common in the USA, it is widely used in Europe and other countries. Some electronic industries in the USA have high spillovers yet apparently perform quite well in terms of dynamic technical efficiency. Markets characterized by high spillovers or their effects on prices fare much better than the same markets populated by fully informed firms. In this respect underestimated spillovers are like subsidies. There is one difference, however. Subsidies by state tend to lower entry barriers and increase the number of viable competitors. But more aggressive R&D investments based on underestimated spillovers increase entry barriers and reduce the number of viable competitors.

In an unregulated market, incentives for R&D are suboptimally low. And these incentives deteriorate with spillovers and the absence of internal appropriability. If the spillovers are substantial, the incentives may simply decline with more concentration. The output of R&D activity has the character of a public good. Firms have low incentives to supply it. But we do not approach the solution to public goods problems by forcing the beneficiaries to pay for it, because that leads to underconsumption and suboptimal use. This suboptimality is a case of market failure.

Risk and uncertainty are another major source of market failure. Risk is associated with information flows, which are either incomplete or uncertain. Decisions based on these information flows give rise to departure from the first best. Consider the investment decision problem. The investor has to evaluate the expected net returns from various alternative projects. But due to the uncertainty of outcomes and the limited existence of markets for insuring risk, the investor may have to resort to suboptimal decisions by resorting to close substitutes as a basis for its estimation of expected probability. Similarly in many developing countries the credit and loan market is not very well developed. As a result small farmers cannot adopt improved farm practices such as fertilizers or irrigation pumps, and this results in suboptimal decisions. In many third world countries the financial market for risk insurance is either nonexistent or exists for large commercial farmers. This type of market incompleteness is the major cause of market failure. A partial answer to this problem is a cooperative subsidy program with state help. This imperfect information has been identified as a major obstacle to the development of small and medium industrial enterprises. These enterprises usually have restricted access to information and thereby encounter great difficulty assessing new innovation in products, processes, and technologies. They also face the reluctance of capital and credit markets to fund their development. Externalities also generate some uncertainty from an innovation or R&D project. Two fields where this happens are knowledge generation and network effects. Owing to knowledge externalities the private returns from engaging in R&D activities are lower than the social benefits, and the market incentives tend to become inefficiently low. In this case state intervention could provide a subsidy to bring the private returns in line with social returns. This would yield optimal and first-best solutions. In markets with network externalities the economic value of a good or service has two parts: the intrinsic value of the good and the value of the "network." The second part is most important in communications technology. Thus, the users of Mac computers are better off if the number of users who purchase Macs increases. This is because the larger the number of Mac users, the greater the demand for compatible software. Such an increase in demand leads to lower prices through scale economies and/or a greater variety of software, which benefits all Mac users. This effect applies to many high-tech markets such as electronics, TV and video recorders, and many communication technologies. The successful NICs in Asia that have achieved high sustained growth rates for the last two decades have exploited the benefits of scale economies of demand through active state support programs and cooperative subsidies. Taiwan's case is most remarkable that it helped the small and medium enterprises avoid the negative consequences of second-best solutions. As a result it achieved high growth with an equalitarian distribution of income, thus providing an important exception to the Kuznets hypothesis.

8.5 Transparency in Information Markets

Market failures are related to imperfect information. A perfectly competitive market is based on five central assumptions: atomicity, product homogeneity, perfect information flows between buyer and sellers, equal access, and free entry. The last three are dependent on the assumption of costless information and its free flow amongst the various agents. In the real world, however, the information flow is neither costless nor fully perfect. The presence of uncertainty and the absence of adequate markets for trading risk tend to complicate matters. This is especially true in three types of markets, e.g., capital market, technology market, and innovation market. Banks and stock market transactions are at the center of the financial system in most developing countries. In general banks are perceived to be more fragile and vulnerable than nonfinancial firms because they tend to have low capital-to-asset ratios (i.e., they are highly leveraged), a low cash-to-asset ratio, and a high ratio of short-term demand deposits to total liabilities. Prudential supervision in many countries has failed to ensure that these fragility ratios remain at reasonable levels. In the USA and other countries the financial crisis and meltdown in 2007–2008 have been caused by the failure of banks and other financial institutions to maintain reasonable caution in advancing subprime home mortgage loans to households who did not have the repaying capacity. A growing body of empirical evidence suggests that key sources of financial fragility and banking sector weakness are microeconomic and institutional failings. These failings include poor management and weakness in the legal framework, inadequate supervision, and perverse incentives. To stem the tide of financial meltdown the US government had to adopt a huge bailout of large banks to the tune of more than 700 billion dollars. Also it had to bail out the insurance giant AIG, which failed miserably in the insurance market.

The failings of the stock market in the recent years, 2007–2009, may be traced to several factors, e.g., premature financial liberalization, inadequate supervision of transactions in hedge funds, large volume of speculative trading, voluminous deals in derivatives without any ceilings or liquidity constraints, and finally the pricing bubbles without the backing of fundamental economic forces. All these factors contribute to the increased riskiness of investor portfolios, which turn into actual losses when a price bubble bursts or the economic downturn occurs very sharply. In such conditions even loans that are fully collateralized can become nonperforming, since the same shock that reduces the borrower's ability to repay may simultaneously reduce the value of the collateral pledged to obtain the loan. For instance, a developer who borrows to invest in real estate and pledges land for collateral would put the lender doubly at risk if property prices experience a sudden collapse. This happened in the US housing market during 2007–2010 as the large-scale default of home mortgage loans intensified the financial instability of the US stock market.

The technology market essentially deals with the creation and dissemination of applied knowledge. R&D investment, applied industrial research, and software development are some examples of this knowledge. The initial cost of creating knowledge or scientific information may be very high, but once it has been acquired its dissemination cost drops significantly. These intrinsic characteristics make knowledge a public good, since it can be shared among an unlimited number of consumers. It generates positive externalities. The presence of these externalities suggests that the level of spending by the private innovator of knowledge creation may be suboptimal because of the difficulties of appropriating the total benefit of the created knowledge. In other words, the market here fails to provide appropriate incentives to knowledge creation. Owing to knowledge externalities the private returns from activities such as R&D are lower than the social benefits, and the market incentives are inefficiently low. Economically justified public intervention would devise a subsidy policy in this situation to bring the private returns in line with the social ones. Among the possible solutions Hausmann and Rodrick (2003) suggested a carrot-and-stick strategy, where the state support may take the form of a subsidy of any kind, e.g., trade protection, soft loans, or provision of venture capital, but on the other side rents that investors receive should be subject to either performance requirements (e.g., export requirements) or close monitoring. The economic policy of the successful NICs in Asia has used both elements of this strategy with great success, while Latin-American policy has used too much of "the carrot" and too little of the "stick." This explains why Latin America has ended up with a considerable degree of inefficiency in its development process compared with the highly growing NICs in Asia.

8.6 Market Power and Dominant Firms

Imperfectly competitive markets offer significant market power to the dominant firms. Such market dominance generates several consequences. First, the dominant firm may have access to a new technology with the first-mover advantage. This advantage may enable the dominant firm to capture excess rents to the detriment of potential entrants and consumers. As an example we may refer to the case of DuPont, which maintained a cost advantage over the rival producers of titanium dioxide. This occurred because it held exclusive patent rights over a lower-cost production process. Even after these patent rights expired DuPont maintained much of that advantage because of the fact that it transformed a first-mover advantage into competitive advantage by utilizing its learning by doing and cost-efficiency from experience. Second, the dominant firm may adopt other strategies when it cannot prevent entry. For instance it can still try to sustain monopoly power by inducing the exit of its rivals. This practice is called predation. This pricing below cost temporarily to injure rival firms and to induce their exit is often called predatory pricing. As an example we may refer to the case of KLM, the dominant airline in the London–Amsterdam route. easyJet encountered this predatory pricing strategy by KLM as soon as it entered this route. Eventually after a court battle this was settled, and the KLM's aggressive price strategy ended. Another source of predatory pricing is the growing markets in this age of globalized trade, where long-term success requires a significant market share from early on. This happened for example in PC operating systems market. Here it is important to start with a good installed base of adopters so that the other developers have an incentive to write software running on the operating systems. Thus, new users get attracted to the operating system, and a sort of snowball effect takes place. Thus, this type of predatory pricing may be successful in that it prevents rivals from attaining the critical market share that is necessary to survive in the market through the optimum scale of operation.

Game theorists have shown that predatory behavior of dominant firms may be profitable if incumbent firms have information about their own costs or market demand that the entrants or the rivals lack. Hence, uncertainty and asymmetry make predation rational. If the entrant is uncertain about the postentry price, then the incumbent's limit pricing strategy can affect the entrant's expectations. An entrant is likely to know less about the incumbent's costs than the incumbent itself does. If so, then by engaging in limit pricing the incumbent dominant firm makes it appear that it has low costs. This will lower the entrant's expectations of postentry profitability and potentially deter it from entering. Some well-known firms such as Walmart and American Airlines enjoy a reputation for toughness earned after a fierce price competition led to the demise of its rivals. Some firms such as Black and Decker and McCormick Spices may announce and advertise a mission to achieve a dominant market share. These announcements may effectively signal to rivals that these firms will do whatever is necessary, even sustain price wars, to secure their share of the market.

Various theoretical models have been developed in the literature characterizing the optimal limit pricing strategy of a dominant firm. Recently Sengupta and Fanchon (2009) have discussed these models and developed a dynamic limit pricing model in which the dominant firm uses price as the control variable so as to maximize the present value of its stream of profits subject to the dynamics of entry described by a state equation that assumes that the response of the fringe (i.e., rival competitors) is captured by a response coefficient growing exponentially with time due to market growth. In this dynamic limit pricing model the dominant firm sets the price, and the fringe firms follow the leader and lower production costs due to newer technology. The dominant firm and the fringe are both profit-maximizing agents and have access to new technology. The dominant firm invests in the new technology and updates it to retain its leadership position.

The dominant firm may also follow an alternative strategy of forcing exit of its rivals. It may use its accumulated retained earnings to buy out the fringe firms when they are successful in their R&D efforts. Such a strategy is feasible in cases where market penetration by the fringe firms is slow. In this situation the dominant firm acquires the extraproductive capacity and access to the incremental innovations of the fringe. Such a strategy might be the only viable strategy available for the dominant firm, if the fringe can protect its innovations with patents. The resulting market structure is then characterized by a large dominant firm and a high concentration ratio for the industry. This may entail a substantial loss of consumer surplus. Such a strategy has been used extensively in high-tech industries such as software development, computer services, and pharmaceuticals. This explains widespread mergers such as Oracle and Microsoft buying out rival or expanding subsidiaries in China, India, and other NICs in Asia.

Finally, we must refer to another long-run strategy of a dominant firm, which is different from a limit pricing or predatory pricing. This is to hold excess capacity or to create excess capacity by innovations for strategic purposes. By holding or creating excess capacity an incumbent dominant firm may affect how potential entrants or rivals view postentry competition and thereby blockade entry. Because the incumbent's excess capacity is sunk, this creates a natural asymmetry. Unlike predatory pricing and limit pricing excess capacity may deter entry even when the entrant possesses complete information about the incumbent's strategic intentions. The dominant incumbent may even decide not to utilize all of its capacity, with the idle capacity serving as a credible commitment that the incumbent will expand output should entry occur. The MNCs in many developing countries have tacitly adopted this strategy. But corrective state policies have also been adopted in many of these countries.

8.7 Concluding Remarks

We have already discussed the recent trend of technology in today's business world. Over the last three decades the economies have undergone a transformation from large-scale material manufacturing to the design and use of new technologies such as software and R&D development. The underlying mechanisms shaping these new technology developments are increasingly characterized by IR. These IR processes are activated by learning by doing and knowledge creation. The process of creative destruction as emphasized by Schumpeter acts as a catalytic agent in this dynamic process. This framework has a most dramatic impact on the market structure, where the globalization and transnational acquisitions tend to increase the role of dominant firms all over the world. This raises the enormous problem of the need to obtain worldwide coordination and also control, since this may easily lead to significant divergences from the first-best competitive solution, if not properly regulated. The worldwide financial crisis in the recent period of 2007–2009 should act as a stark reminder.

Chapter 9
Growth Policy

Modern growth theory emphasizes a deliberate state policy to promote economic growth. Although Solow's model used a neoclassical production function where competitive markets played an optimizing role, long-run economic growth was determined by technological progress, which was assumed to be exogenous. Markets and state policy cannot influence technological progress. Modern endogenous growth theory rejected this paradigm of Solow model. It used a broader concept of technology and its progress. This concept is innovation, which was emphasized by Schumpeter in his dynamic theory of economic growth. The modern concept of innovation and its efficiency is much broader than that introduced by Schumpeter. In particular it includes various forms of knowledge capital, learning by doing, and managerial skills with organizational learning. These forms of innovations are becoming more and more important in today's world. These modern forms of innovations have three important characteristics. First, the designs and use of technologies through software and computer networking have introduced increasing returns (IR) processes. These have significantly challenged the competitive equilibrium paradigms of the neoclassical world. The ability to constantly reconfigure business relations via networking with other firms in foreign countries was not originally considered to be part of firm-specific advantage affecting the propensity of firms to compete in foreign markets. Recent success of Asian NICs has acknowledged the role of foreign linkages as critical sources of their competitive advantage. Second, the models of evolutionary economics have shown the importance of dynamic capability theory and the concept of core competence through organizational learning by doing. Through these measures the successful firms can sustain their competitive advantages despite the fact that competition according to orthodox theory should eliminate these advantages. The original Schumpeterian innovation did not elaborate the precise characteristics of the creative process in the model of creative destruction. Dividing the production process into increasingly simpler elements, e.g., miniaturization, is a continuous discovery process yielding new knowledge rather than being a choice between a series of given alternatives as assumed by neoclassical production theory. Finally, modern evolutionary economics emphasizes many types and dimensions of innovations related to the endogenous dynamics of competitive advantage. By implication some

J. Sengupta, *Understanding Economic Growth: Modern Theory and Experience*,

DOI 10.1007/978-1-4419-8026-7_9,

types of innovations may change the distribution of competitive advantages among firms more than, and in different ways from, other types of innovations. Innovations, which are "competence-enhancing," are more important than those that are "competence-destroying," since they generate a cumulative process of induced innovations. One innovation leads to another as in the miniaturization technology and its transfer across firms and industries. Thus, the internal resources of the firms are critical to sustaining a steady rate of growth in today's economy. They maintain and enhance the competence perspective, which is about the creation, maintenance, and renewal of competitive advantage in terms of the internal resources of the firm.

The resource-based theory of endogenous growth links strategic resources of firms and industries to the productivity growth, which in turn reduces unit cost and expands the market. The neoclassical model stressed the physical side of resources as inputs to the material production process such as manufacturing, but the modern theory emphasizes the human side, the creative side of knowledge capital. It improves efficiency through knowledge transfer, creating new products and services through new ventures in bioengineering, pharmaceuticals, and new sources of solar and other alternative forms of energy.

Economic growth involves two sides. One is the output side with consumption as the end use. The other is the cost side, which discusses the cost implications of various resources used in the production and distribution processes of the economy. Any discussion of growth policy must begin with an assessment of the resource costs incurred in any rapid development process. These resource costs may take many forms, of which the following are most important.

1. Cost of energy
2. Cost of learning by doing
3. Cost of institutional change
4. Cost of debt crisis

9.1 Costs of Growth

We discuss in brief some of the above costs of development. Rapid growth has some inherent price in the form of various structural and institutional adjustments. These adjustments involve both private and social costs. Markets do not always reflect these costs, and market failures cause a strategic divergence of private and social benefits from economic growth. Two important questions arise in this framework. The first is regarding the effectiveness of state policy in reducing some of the costs. The experiences of the successful NICs in Asia provide some examples in this regard. The policies of China, Taiwan, and India are particularly relevant here. Second, is it possible to repeat the successful growth experiences of the NICs in East Asia without necessarily incurring the social costs of development?

We attempt here to provide some answers to these questions in more theoretical terms, frequently referring to the examples of China, Taiwan, and India.

These examples are selected for two reasons. The first is that they represent a diversity of political institutions. China's entry into WTO in 2001 has opened up its liberalization drive toward a market economy so as to improve its position in the world competitive markets. In spite of its population problem India continues to play a dynamic role as a next tier NIC in Asia. It is most likely to grow further in the IT and communications fields. Second, these countries are showing consistent economic strength in the area of information technology, which forms the cornerstone of modern endogenous growth theory.

9.2 Energy Policy

The stock of natural resources is of two types: renewable and nonrenewable. Renewable resources such as solar energy get their supply renewed by nature, although pollutions and carbon emissions can limit their supply somewhat. The nonrenewable resources such as coal, petroleum, and minerals are depleted over time. Most of energy supply in the form of power and electricity is derived from the supply of nonrenewable resources that are limited in supply. Both land and energy generate a lag in the long-run growth rate of an economy. It is sometimes called a "drag" due to diminishing returns associated with the limits supply of the nonrenewable resources. In the short and medium term, however, land can be transformed into more productive uses, and energy in the form of power can speed up the process of growth of the medium and small industries. Other forms of energy such as nuclear and hydroelectric power can help the growth of heavy industries.

In endogenous growth models the renewable resources are the source of constant or increasing returns. As part of social infrastructure these resource inputs enter into the aggregate production function as helping the productivity of labor and physical capital to grow over time. Power supply as a form of nonrenewable resource is essential to industrial investment and the technology sector. In modern growth theory, technology is sometimes measured by a proxy variable such as an index of energy value. If economic efficiency is key to sustained long-run growth, then it is most important to obtain an optimal use of energy as the power source of industrial development.

Rapid growth of NICs in Asia over the last few decades would have been impossible without an effective use of energy. Maintaining efficiency in energy use has been central to economic growth in China, Taiwan, and Korea. Large FDI in these countries have been so successfully employed because of adequate supply of power and well-structured infrastructure.

Two features of energy consumption for industrial growth have to be noted. One is energy demand for the general-purpose technology (GPT) growth. Most of the rapid growth in NICs in Asia is attributable to these technologies, which are technologies that have a wide scope for improvement and elaboration and are applicable over a broad range of uses. These GPT can be machine tools such as lathe, or new materials with new properties, or more efficient ways of producing, transmitting, and utilizing energy to do industrial work. Second, there is the "*rebound effect*" in energy consumption, both direct and indirect. Economists have recognized that a range of mechanisms, commonly grouped under the heading of rebound effects, may reduce the size of energy savings attempted by energy-efficient improvements adopted by governments. This may apply in particular to new technologies such as steam engines in the nineteenth century, which significantly improved economic productivity as well as energy efficiency. When these rebound effects are large and significant, they can have far-reaching implications for energy and climate policy. While cost-effective improvements in energy efficiency would improve welfare and increase industrial output, they could in some cases provide an ineffective and counterproductive means of tackling climate worsening.

Economic trends in China, Taiwan, and recently India clearly indicate that the rebound effects are likely to increase over time. Ecological economists have emphasized a balanced approach to counter the adverse effects of large rebound effects. While technological progress increases thermodynamic efficiency in energy use, it increases the carbon dioxide emissions. But the introduction of a carbon tax would have an adverse effect on economic growth. Thus, a balance is needed between the quantity and quality of growth. Efficiency has to be combined with sufficiency and sustenance. A measure of sufficiency is to limit the consumption of goods and services either to better satisfy health and environmental needs or to improve the quality of life. One has to recognize that sustainability of growth is incompatible with the environmental degradation through pollution and adverse rebound effects. The latter reflect the cost of economic growth, and the competitive market system may fail to incorporate this cost in their pricing structure and hence the need for corrective state policy.

It is useful to review the present status and future goals of energy policy in China. Real GDP at 1995 prices has grown at an average annual rate of over 9%, which is substantially higher than the record for other developing countries. At the same time population in China has grown 1.2% per year. Total energy supply increased from 493 mtoe (million tons of oil equivalent) in 1980 to 905 mtoe in 1999 by an average increase of over 3.2% per year. China accounts for roughly 10% of total world energy consumption. Since 1979 the rate of growth in China's oil demand exceeded the rate of growth in oil production, and China is now a net importer of crude oil. Rapid economic growth in China has led to an increase in oil demand from 2.1 million barrels per day in 1990 to about 4.4 million barrels per day in 1999, an average annual increase of 4.0%. At the current rate of economic growth, its oil demand is projected to increase by about 3.8 million barrels per day by 2010 and up to 11.1 million barrels per day in 2020. Also China is increasingly becoming a major factor in international natural gas trade. Current production of natural gas in China is about one trillion cubic feet. It has a substantial supply of gas resources in the Sichuan and Tarim basin, as well as in the western South China sea. Still it is unlikely that China can meet its projected natural gas needs without turning to imports.

In 1996 China unveiled a national plan to attain around a third of its energy needs through international exploration and acquisition activities, by outbidding countries such as Venezuela, Sudan, Iran, and Kazakhstan.

One dismal consequence of the large share of coal in total energy consumption in Asia is the large carbon emissions. In 2000 China's carbon emissions accounted for almost 40% (775 million metric tons) of total Asian emissions and 76% of carbon emissions from China was from coal use. Another case is India; in 2000 its carbon emissions accounted for about 13% (253 million metric tons) of total Asian emissions, 66% of which was from coal use. Altogether China and India account for roughly 52% for all emissions in Asia, yet per capita emissions are 0.61 metric tons per capita in China and 0.25 in India. These are far below the world average of 0.61 metric tons per capita. The OECD Report (2008) estimates that gross carbon emissions in China will most likely exceed those in the USA by 2011, making China the simple largest emitter of carbon dioxide in the world. India is not far behind.

Three types of policy reforms are called for in China and India. One is to reduce the high degree of inefficiency in production and transformation of energy resource. Besides technological and skill deficiencies, there exist glaring deficiencies in management and regulatory systems and a general lack of financial incentives to improve. Liberalization of energy markets and improving efficiency through learning by doing would provide the right strategy. Second, both China and India, and to some extent Taiwan, have inefficient end use of energy. This is largely due to their lack of access o appropriate up-to-date technologies. Though China has adopted many reforms in the incentive structure, still much remains to be done. India has to be more vigorous in following the Chinese strategy. Finally, one needs a balanced policy for controlling pollution through the transformation and end use of coal. Coal will continue to provide more than 50% of China's primary energy supply in the next decade. For India the trend is similar. The use of clean-coal technology and substitution of coal by natural gas and primary electricity requires a sustained program of incentives and capital investment. State planning for this goal is vital, and liberalization of the energy market can greatly help. In China as in India there exist several obstacles to liberalization as follows:

1. Outright resistance over giving up government control.
2. Legal and institutional resistance. Since China lacks an independent judiciary and appropriate laws on competitive markets and property rights, an efficient system of contracts is unenforceable. The transaction costs for changing the state-controlled institutions are very exorbitant. In India there is great political resistance due to the existence of multiple political parties forming a very weak central government.
3. Incremental and piecemeal reforms in the energy sector. Both China and India have two strategy options. One is to continue control and ownership over most of the energy sector, introducing reforms at the margin. But this may be very inadequate for sustaining a long-run rising trend in economic growth. The second strategy is to continue the current pattern of energy policy but at the same time adopt and implement a coherent long-term strategy for the progressive liberalization of the energy sector.

Now we discuss a few points about the energy policy in India, since it is going to play a major role in the next decade. First, India has vast untapped hydroelectric power potential. Estimates place this potential at 64,000 MW of which only 37%

has been utilized as of 2008. Only about one-fifth of India's total electricity generation comes from hydroelectric power plants. Other alternative energy sources such as solar and wind have great prospect. The Indian Planning Commission has set up the objective to achieve 10% of all additional electric capacity coming from renewable energy sources by 2012; the Indian Renewable Energy Development Agency has started implementing appropriate policy measures. Measures of liberalization and developing appropriate market structures with incentives are urgently called for. Second, the Indian government needs to focus on reforms on the transmission and distribution system in the power sector. Lowering power costs, reducing huge losses in the transmission and distribution system, and improving managerial skills are the key components of a progressive reform policy. Finally, India has taken some initial steps in improving efficiency in the energy sector through market-based reforms. The Energy Conservation Act has been passed in 2001, and a Bureau of Energy Efficiency has been established. However, the reform measures so far adopted by this Bureau have been very slow, weak, and relatively inefficient. Much remains to be done.

9.3 Learning by Doing

Learning by doing in endogenous growth theory usually refers to the positive side of industry growth. It refers to the stock of cumulative experience and knowledge capital that enhances the core competence and dynamic flexibility of a firm. Arrow's original concept referred to the large productivity gains in the aircraft industry in the USA due to this cumulative experience of human capital termed as "learning by doing." However, it has a negative side due to the various costs associated with it. It is useful here to discuss some of these cost concepts associated with learning by doing.

The learning process involves several forms. The first is to learn by imitation. At the initial stage FDI in East-Asian countries allowed this opportunity. Some of these countries imitated the new up-to-date technology and improved it. Japan consistently followed this practice and increased its competitive power. Taiwan, China, and recently India all are still following this step. But improving is the key item for industrial growth. Second, learning on the job and improving the skills of human capital have direct impact on industry growth. The modern endogenous growth theory emphasized the dynamic role of spillover effect by which industrial knowledge shifts from the advanced countries to the developing ones. To catch this effect the industries in the developing countries have to practice organizational learning and management, and dynamic flexibility in their decision making. Countries such as China and Taiwan have adopted the policy of sending their residents to the USA and other developed OECD countries for a period of learning at the colleges and universities and bringing them back for domestic employment. Japan was very successful in this method. Third, improving the domestic level of technical and engineering education and tapping the hidden resource of human capital also provide a valued learning resource for intensifying economic growth. Fourth, stepping up the general level of education all around the country also helps indirectly the resource base of learning to increase. The government's spending on education at all levels and also on research in new areas such as solar and renewable energy or agricultural research provides an important strategy for augmenting the learning process. Finally, management skills in organizational learning are most essential. Hence, the state policy should support and encourage the management education and research activity in the country. Problems of coordination and organization inefficiency are two most basic problems that hinder economic growth. The high level of success in the NICs in Asia has been achieved in part through reducing this inefficiency of organizations and coordination problems. Opening up to the world competitive markets has helped greatly, but still the bureaucratic inefficiency and bottlenecks are very significant.

In 2006 China adopted a 15-year Medium-to-Long-Term Plan for the Development of Science and Technology (MLP), which sets the target for China to become an "innovation-oriented society" by 2020 and a world leader in science and technology by 2020. High-speed growth in China over the last three decades exceeding 9% per year on average has created problems of overinvestment, excessive dependence on exports, inefficient utilization of human and other resources, and the devastating effect on environment. From a growth strategy standpoint, the MLP of China can be viewed as a critical statement on the three basic costs of rapid development and how to reduce them. First, in spite of China's rapid growth of GNP its record of innovation in commercial technologies has been very unremarkable. Instead its dependence on foreign technology had grown consistently over the past two decades, since the state policy favored multinational companies to transfer up to date technology in return for export market opportunities. But with its entry into WTO foreign corporations can no longer transfer advanced technologies needed by more sophisticated Chinese companies. Second, China's technological capabilities are also failing to meet its national needs in such areas as energy, environmental quality, and public health. Finally, the state of China's science and technology had their disappointments. Many of China's best and brightest have tough career opportunities in the USA and abroad, despite the array of incentives offered by the state. It is instructive to consider some Chinese statistics here. The gross expenditures on R&D have grown from 6.65 (US $ billion) in 1998 to 18.61 in 2003 and 36.79 in 2006, but as a ratio to GDP (%) it raised from 0.69 in 1998 to 1.31 in 2003 and 1.42 in 2006. The scientists and engineers engaged in R&D rose from 485.5 (in 1,000 person-year) in 1998 to 1,224 in 2006. Graduate student enrollment rose from 198.9 in 1998 (in 1,000) to 1,100 in 2006. Similar figures for undergraduate enrollment rose from 3.41 in 1998 (in billions) to 17.39 in 2006. The MLP has identified its priority areas, which induce 11 broad "key areas" relating to national needs such as energy, IT industry, transportation, and national defense and eight areas of "frontier technology" such as biotechnology, IT, new materials, laser, aerospace, and advanced energy from ocean and sun. The private enterprise sector has been given some preference in the MLP. However, one recent survey by government indicated that

Chinese enterprises are not taking R&D activities very seriously. According to this survey report submitted to the Chinese Consultative Conference, only 25% of the large and medium-sized enterprises have established R&D departments. Criticisms of the inclusion of many so-called megaprograms in the MLP surfaced in 2004, when a group of prominent US-based Chinese life scientists complained to Premier Wen Jinbao that the state funding of the biosciences in the 863 and 973 programs was biased, inefficient, and bureaucratically controlled.

There have been, however, some encouraging signs for the future. One aspect of MLP implementation is the encouragement of China's wealthy local governments to invest more in science and technology. Spending on science and technology rose from 29% of total government expenditure in 1995 to more than 39% in 2005. This trend has been rising over the next 5 years. Eight of China's wealthier provinces now spend considerably more on science and technology as a percentage of total government spending than the national average of 2.08%, e.g., Shanghai 4.78%, Zhejian 3.95%, Guandong 3.66%, Beijing 3.55%, and Fujian 2.29%. This surge in local government expenditure on science and technology is generating new major funding sources for R&D and new cooperative projects between the central government and the local governments. Second, despite the slow pace, science and technology strategy is rapidly advancing in some new areas. For example in nanotechnology that emphasizes the miniaturization process in IT, 29 projects have been selected with a total fund of RMB 262 million allocated. One has to note also that the central planners have adopted several efficiency measures to improve the management of the megaengineering projects. Here there is the need to strike a proper balance between the indigenous efforts at research and innovation with global technology flows and knowledge development.

Taiwan's growth experience is more remarkable than that of China. It excelled in ICT (information and communication technology). Since 1995 it became a major global center of electronic system design, manufacturing, and logistics. One basic index of Taiwan's technological achievements is its ranking among US patent recipients. In 1980 it ranked 21st, by 1990 it reached 11th, and in 1995 it ranked 7th. In 2005 it was among the first four. Today Taiwan leads China in the ICT sector. Many Taiwanese companies and their components are manufactured for original equipment manufacturers, so most ICT goods are exported. This accounts for about 33% of total exports. Taiwan's computer hardware production rose from $19.5 million in 1995 to $48.0 million in 2000. The offshore hardware production changed from 82.2% growth rate in 1995 to about 35.3% in 2000. Taiwan is China's fourth largest source of FDI; this investment accounted for only 7.76% of China's cumulative total FDI, but part of Hong Kong's investment in China is actually from Taiwan. The performance record of Taiwan's computer software production is also most remarkable.

For example the total computer software production in Taiwan rose from 48,893 (NT $ million) in 1996 to 118,728. If the total is broken into product market, project market, and service market, then the changes are as follows: 25,545–57,119, 14,953–33,520, and 8,395–28,089. Annual growth rates for 1999–2000 were 24.40% for the total and 16.95, 25.00, 42.00%, respectively, for the products, projects, and services.

The Taiwanese government has provided subsidies, loans, and tax breaks for private R&D efforts, but unlike Japan and South Korea Taiwan's industrial growth was highly decentralized and technology widely diffused across medium- and small-sized firms. In the early 1990s the R&D expenditure from the public sector accounted for more than half of the total R&D expenditure. By 1999 the proportion of private R&D expenditure had risen to 62.1%. The electrical and electronic machinery industry had the highest ratio of R&D spending to sales of any manufacturing industry.

One problem in the current trend in R&D spending is that almost all of R&D spending is for applied research and technology development, none is for basic research. For example the electrical and electronic machinery industry allocates about 75% of R&D spending to technology development and 25% to applied research. Figures for the information service industry are 50 and 50, respectively. In the long run this may raise the issue if Taiwan's high growth rate can be sustained at all. Technologies as innovation are of two types: general purpose (GPT) and specific purpose (SPT). GPTs are sometimes called transforming or enabling technologies. These GPTs have major impacts on the social and economic growth structures. SPTs are incremental innovations that help diffuse the modern technology across the medium-and small-sized industries, but unlike the GPTs they have much more limited impact on economic growth. Taiwan's excellence is mostly in SPTs, but for the future it has to improve its record in the area of GPTs or enabling technologies. Hence, the need is greater for basic research in the long run.

An important channel of learning by doing in Taiwan comes through its widespread participation in the world market. Its government has supported and facilitated inward investment and technology transfer by helping domestic companies to develop specialized expertise, identify export opportunities, and exploit those opportunities. Note that overall Taiwan imports more technology than it exports. The electrical and electronic machinery industry accounts for about 75% of total technology import and export values, respectively.

The example of Taiwan shows that India needs to adopt an active policy of technology diffusion as in the Taiwan model. The tremendous externality benefits of the spillover technology associated with international R&D investment need to be captured and adopted by India's private sector. Various management and engineering institutes have a direct role to play here.

Sengupta (2005) has discussed in some detail the important lessons it can learn from the successful growth experiences of the NICs in East Asia. In particular it can follow the Taiwanese model in several respects. First, the Taiwanese government has actively promoted inward investment and technology transfer by helping local companies to develop specialized capabilities, seek out export opportunities and exploit them. India could learn so much from this policy of active cooperation with the private sector. Second, both China and Taiwan have emphasized inward investment and technology transfer by helping local companies to develop specialized capabilities, seek out export opportunities and exploit them. Taiwan's ICT manufacturing has moved from being a labor-intensive to being a technology-intensive industry. This transition is facilitated by building human capital and skill development through learning by doing. Taiwan's Constitution Article 164 proclaims that no less than 15% of the national budget shall be allocated to education and science and so shall 20% of the provincial budget and 25% of the county budget. The UNESCO estimates show that Taiwan has more engineering graduates than other industrial countries such as the USA and Germany. In terms of number of engineering graduates per 10,000 population, the estimates for 1989 are as follows.

Taiwan	4.00	South Korea	6.70
USA	2.70	Germany	1.55
China	1.42	India	0.34

The estimates for 2006 have exceeded 5.90. It is clear that Taiwan's record is more impressive compared to China and India. Recently the International Management Development Institute conducted a survey (2008) among the Asian NICs, and Taiwan with Singapore and South Korea are in the top in science and technology education.

Taiwan's excellence in technology learning by doing has spread from both general-purpose (GPT) and specific-purpose technologies (SPT). While GPTs are enabling or transforming technologies, the SPTs are incremental technologies. Both share some common characteristics. First, they both diffuse throughout the economy and evolve into more complex technologies. This increases scale efficiency dramatically. Second, they generate more learning by doing through the Schumpeterian process of cumulative accumulation of experience and creative destruction. As quality improves, new products emerge and new process technologies emerge. This is very similar to the rebound effect we analyzed in energy policy.

The cumulative process of industry growth in Taiwan taking advantage of the GPTs and the process of learning by doing may be grouped into several categories as follows:

1. ICT industries: This category is most important, and it produces the largest number of US patents. This includes computer, telecommunications, and related technologies, which are driving the current ICT revolution.
2. Power delivery systems: This includes steam engine, electricity, and the internal combustion engine.
3. Material engineering: This includes new materials such as polymer, computer chips, and miniature technology. These generate new products and new uses for the industry and the consumer.
4. Transportation systems: This includes aircraft, motor vehicles, three-masted sailing ship, and high-speed locomotive technology.
5. Organizational technology: This includes mass production and flexible manufacturing, which have been most intensively used by Toyota and hence known as Toyotaism.

As each new GPT diffuses through the economy, it generates a research program for business entrepreneurs to apply and develop new products and also improve old ones. These in turn create other new opportunities and so on in a chain reaction over next decades. For instance Taiwan's innovators have found myriad ways to use electronic chips. As the power and reliability of chips have increased, new industrial ways are discovered. R&D and the learning by doing have helped Taiwan develop other enabling technologies. The impact on the incremental innovations through SPTs has been equally remarkable. Thus, the most dramatic effect of improvement in power supply came not from a fall in the price of power but in the making of possible new products and new processes that were not technically available with steam engines. This impact caused a dramatic increase in labor productivity in all steps of manufacturing production, from the assembly line to flexible manufacturing.

One direct impact of learning by doing is through the R&D capital. Sengupta (2005) has discussed in some detail the growth experience of the successful NICs in Asia and compared India's record. The following estimates are derived from the tram log cost function for the whole economy, which show the elasticity of cost to R&D capital stock:

	1978–1985	1990–1997	2000–2007
Taiwan	0.0087	0.001	0.0006
Korea	0.015	0.081	0.075
Singapore	0.026	0.021	0.020

Here GDP at factor cost is used as a measure of cost. This shows the high degree of cost-efficiency achieved by the Taiwanese economy. Since the cost elasticity is less than one for all these three countries, this suggests that there are significant increasing returns to scale in these countries. The impact of increasing returns to scale is more pronounced for Taiwan than for Korea and Singapore.

There are several lessons for India's economic policy for growth that can be learned from Taiwan and Korea. One has to note that in Schumpeter's innovation process, imitation first and then improvement rather than inventions can provide an important source of growth. The Japanese firms that excel today in world markets have historically gained time and cost advantages in imitation due to their acquisition of the know-how of foreign competitors. Most comparative advantages came not from internal technology but from external technology bought or copied from competitors. According to a recent report (2006) of the US Academy of Sciences, in nearly 300 cases of technology research links between the USA and Japanese companies more than 90% involved transfer of US technology to Japan. In Japan companies take about 25% less time and spend about 50% less money in carrying out an incremental innovation (SPT) because of their use of externally borrowed technology. This way Japan avoids much of the costs of the first mover in the field. Taiwan has also followed this practice very successfully. India needs to develop this strategy.

Equally important is the need for India to adopt an active policy of technology diffusion, when technology is viewed in its broadest sense as the Schumpeterian innovation. It involves international collaboration in R&D and FDI with USA and other global partners. The spillover benefits of international R&D investment need to be captured by Indian entrepreneurs. On the domestic front diffusion must involve induced investment so that competitive efficiency can be promoted through appropriate market incentives. One must note here that governments cannot create competitive industries, only firms and industries can. Governments can only shape or influence the institutional structure for industrial development. The best example is the strategy adopted by the Japanese government, which has been so successful in fostering its growth. This strategy is currently followed very successfully by Taiwan, South Korea, and Singapore. What the Japanese government did is to encourage early demand, develop cooperation policies for adopting frontier technologies, and speed up the process of improving, upgrading, and developing new incremental innovations.

It is useful to analyze the performance of the IT sector in India, as it is going to play a dynamic role in future growth. Two aspects need a close review. One is to analyze the source of comparative advantage for India's exports in IT-based products and services, which are rising very rapidly over the last decade. A second aspect is to reduce the gap between the current IT experience in India and the necessary competence required. Taiwan's model and experience offer here important lessons. First, Taiwan's production of IT output fueled her impressive economic growth at the average annual rate of 7% in the last two decades. Its total IT output grew from less than US $100 million in 1980 to more than $35 billion in 1999. By comparison India's exports of IT services were $1,085 million. In 2000 it rose to $4,500 million. It has still a long way to go. Today Taiwan receives more US patents per capita than any other Asian NICs and ranks ahead of all the G7 countries except the USA and Japan. Two major factors are important. One is the active state policy of rapid transfer of public (state-funded) research and technology know-how to the private sector and the creation of a domestic VC industry influenced by the Silicon Valley model in the USA. Second, the agglomeration and scale effects flowed from the large infusion of entrepreneurial and managerial talents from the USA, which provided important linkages to the latest technology and the world technology market. These forces were instrumental in shifting Taiwan to the technological frontier in the manufacturing of ICs (integrated circuits), PCs, and related components. The contrast with the Indian scene is very revealing. During 1985–1995 India's R&D spending averaged around 1% of GNP, of which 80% was in the government sector. In 2006 the share was still around 75%. India's private sector accounts for less than 15% of total R&D expenditure. Even then this private sector R&D is limited to a handful of industries such as defense, electrical equipment, and pharmaceuticals. Technology diffusion is most limited with regard to the search for technological services. The interactions of private firms and technology institutions are also very limited in India.

India's domestic IT outsourcing, consulting, and systems integration are growing very strongly now from 2006 onward, on average approximately 18.8% annually, and have gone through a major turning point, making the transition from the emergence phase to the growth phase. One has to pay attention now to several costs of development due to stiff competition worldwide and the NICs in Asia such as Taiwan and China. First, India's continuing success in the offshore service market will generate significant stresses in the domestic market as the competitors compete for junior and experienced skilled personnel. Second, India is very poor in project and risk management skills for package implementations. Here non-Indian multinational vendors would surely win a significantly higher share of medium-to-large outsourcing deals.

Two recent policy measures for the IT sector are important. One is the influence of venture capital that is having a growing influence on innovation and technology involving all four stages: idea generation, start-up, growth, and exit. One important venture capital fund in India is known as "National Venture Fund for Software and IT Industry." It is a 10-year fund setup to help small ventures to achieve rapid growth and to maintain global competitiveness. But compared to the Taiwanese model, its utilization rate is very uneven. Second, the Indian government has introduced the Information Technology Act, announcing a policy to permit the entry of private ventures to enter the international market. However, the pace of liberalization is very slow, uneven, and at times inefficient.

Sengupta and Neogi (2009) have discussed the importance of some dynamic strategies in the Indian software industry based on three Cs: competitive advantage, comparative advantage, and core competence in knowledge creation and diffusion. They found that India ranks far lower than China and Taiwan in terms of its rank in three Cs. Software exports from India mainly take three forms (1) software services such as consultancy, (2) support of software packaging developed abroad, and (3) electronic bookkeeping and data entry. All these forms are highly labor-intensive, and India faces stiff competition from six countries, China, Singapore, Taiwan, Ireland, Mexico, and the Philippines, according to a World Bank study. India's record of software package exports is also very poor. This type of exports is less than 3% in 2006, whereas China and Mexico exceed 25%. It is clear that India needs to shift its global strategy from servicing to software package development. This also calls for developing networks and effective alliances with US and Japanese counterparts so that appropriate market niches can be set up worldwide.

9.4 Cost of Institutional Reforms

Growth is essentially institutional change. Both economic and extraeconomic institutions must change if economic growth has to continue. Economic institutions include for example the market and the banks. Extraeconomic institutions comprise for example governance in terms of laws and regulations and the bureaucratic systems. Both types of institutions are essential for economic growth. The neoclassical theory emphasized the competitiveness of markets as central to economic growth and ignored the roles of governance and the legal framework. Recent developments in evolutionary models of growth have made us aware today of the important role of democracy and social conventions and the regulatory power of political and social institutions. We would discuss here some of their costs and benefits and refer to the experience of rapidly growing countries of Southeast Asia.

The dynamics of industry growth, technology, and innovations have a dramatic impact on the current economic growth of nations, significantly changing the market structure and world trade. It has challenged the competitive equilibrium paradigm and their guiding principles. In the world of GPT and SPT innovations and spillover effects, various forms of noncompetitive market structures have evolved in recent times. Modern industrial economies have undergone a transformation from large-scale material manufacturing to the design of incremental innovations and software technology characterized by increasing returns (IR). Dynamic flexibility and managerial competence are more critically needed in this framework. Mergers and acquisitions across national borders have expanded the multinational enterprises (MNEs). The knowledge embodied in new processes, products, and proprietary technology provides the MNEs with the advantages necessary to overcome the disadvantages associated with foreign activity. The ability to constantly recognize business relations via networking with other firms in foreign countries has been used as a dynamic strategy by the high-growth countries of Southeast Asia such as Taiwan, Singapore, and China. The internationalization of firms dominated by IR process has been strongly and positively related to the intensity of networking and collaborative activities as recent empirical studies have shown. A recent empirical study by Nachum (2002) has shown that entrepreneurship networking and flexible organizational structure have helped MNEs develop dynamic capabilities as discussed in evolutionary growth theory and that they enhance the MNE's competitive edge over other competitors. The NICs in Asia have exploited this networking strategy to develop their organizational flexibility and efficiency. Taiwan, Singapore, and South Korea are clear examples. India has lagged behind in this respect considerably.

However, one should note some costs associated with the multinationality and the IR process. In many developing economies such as India or Indonesia, the MNEs have acquired the position of dominant forms in the IT and other technology-intensive sectors and have indirectly caused stumbling blocks for the domestic firms to enter the market and adopt new technology. Second, the culture of domestic innovations has suffered badly. This is evident in the IT strategy followed in India, where there is very little networking between the domestic research and technology institutes and the private sector business and its emphasis on R&D is very low compared to Taiwan or Singapore. A need for drastic policy reforms is urgent here.

Besides market reforms, banking is another area where reform is essential for economic growth. This is so because of two basic reasons. One is the credit and loan facility, which helps private investment to grow. Good monetary policy is, therefore, essential for economic development. The financial crisis of 2007–2009 affecting the USA and the world economy is basically due to the failure of the banking system and the economy-wide credit policies. A second reason is that the networking strategy by the domestic banking sector can set up very profitable links with banks abroad and this facilitates the expansion of the world market. The successful NICs in China have been greatly helped by their liberalization drive in the banking sector and its networking capabilities.

Since its entry into WTO in December 2001, China has started liberalization of its banking sector in a systematic fashion. Still the government control on the banking system is pervasive so much that the return on nonperforming assets of the state-controlled banks is negative and competitive inefficiency is significant. Taiwan's record is exemplary. It has very successfully set up networking links abroad, and the international credit system works very smoothly for Taiwan.

It is useful to consider India's experience on this regard, since it is one of the major stumbling blocks to a good monetary policy that is essential for growth. We may refer here to two important research studies, one by Sengupta and Sahoo (2006) and the other by Sengupta and Neogi (2009). The first studies the scale and scope economies and capacity utilization in the Indian banking industry over the 5-year period of 1997–2001 based on 78 commercial banks with each having three or more branches. The second study analyzed a sample of 68 commercial banks for a period of 9 years (1997–2005). Both studies applied the linear programming method of Pareto efficiency, also known as data envelopment analysis (DEA), and analyzed the impact of state liberalization policies.

The first study compared the performance of nationalized (i.e., state-owned) and private banks and found the following results. First, the private and foreign banks enjoy more scale economies than unnationalized banks. Second, the private and foreign banks utilize their capacity more compared to nationalized banks. Two reasons for the higher level of excess capacity in nationalized banks over the private banks can be given. The first is that before deregulation in 1992 the banking industry was characterized by an oligopoly structure protected by government regulations; no competition existed. Second, the consolidation of nationalized banks was not strong enough to eliminate excess capacity. Thus, irrespective of ownership and size the Indian banking sector is characterized by large excess capacity. Some examples are as follows:

Capacity utilization rate	1999–2001
Large	0.3814
Medium	0.2814
Small	1.1140

The empirical results also show large economies of scope, larger for the nationalized banks. Here there exists a great scope for banks to generate more returns by a judicious process of integration and coordination of their loan activities. For example banks with higher percentage of performing loan assets could on average increase their output by 31% and inefficient banks by 48%.

The second study used a sample of 27 public sector banks, 28 domestic private sector banks, and 13 foreign banks for a period of 9 years (1997–2005). Several important results are derived. First of all the percentage of public sector commercial banks suffer from significant diminishing returns to scale. This is largely due to inoptimal size. By contrast the foreign banks suffer less from scale inefficiency. The Indian government's future goal to restructure large nationalized banks by merging them to create a few very large banks is likely to aggravate scale efficiency.

The private sector banks performed well and exhibited increasing returns to scale. Second, we measured economies due to learning by doing by running log-linear regressions for each year for the banks of different ownership and for only those banks found to be technically efficient by the DEA model. The regression function is of the form

$$\log \mathrm{AC} = f(\log \mathrm{CO}, \log W),$$

where AC represents the average cost, CO denotes the average cumulative output over 3 years, and W represents labor costs. Total cost here is the sum of operating expense and interest costs. Output is defined as total assets net of fixed assets. If the coefficient of cumulative output is less than one, then economies due to learning by doing exist. If it is greater than one, then diseconomies prevail. The results for 2003 and 2005 are as follows in terms of the regression coefficient of cumulative output.

Coefficient of cumulative output		
	2003	2005
All banks	−1.16*	−0.25*
Public banks	−0.37**	−0.38**
Private banks	−0.020**	−0.09
Foreign banks	−0.05	−0.53

* and ** denote significant t-values at 5 and 1%, respectively

Overall we can say that cumulative experience is helping all banks reduce unit costs. The coefficients for the foreign banks are not statistically significant, and in most cases they operate at optimum average costs.

However, our study did not include two important deficiencies of Indian commercial banks. One is their networking deficiency with respect to other international transactions. The other is their need for bringing more competitive efficiency in their operations. One of the critical reasons why the technology market is so poorly developed is the regulatory framework underlying the Indian banking system. Policy decisions of the Reserve Bank of India need to be more progressive and more technology-oriented. Growth of R&D innovation and technology diffusion have been very slow in India. NIC countries such as Taiwan and Singapore have made great progress. India needs to follow their example. After its entry into WTO even China has made great strides in the financial reform and banking policies.

Cost of inefficiency in governance and lack of suitable progressive economic laws favorable to sustaining competitive efficiency have acted as great deterrence to economic growth. In spite of a totalitarian government structure China has embraced the free market strategy in all its components such as the stock market, entry of large flows of FDI, liberalization of tax and fiscal policies favoring industrial growth in the coastal areas, and promoting the growth of joint ventures and foreign venture capital. It has also adopted some safeguards against the dominance of MNEs in China. Taiwan's record is much superior. It has stressed economic efficiency in all its economic reforms, and it has achieved remarkable success in earning new US patents for software and other innovations.

The inefficiency in governance can be analyzed in several ways. One is the transactions cost approach emphasized by the Coase theorem and North's theory. As North (1990) argued that in a world where there are no transaction costs and increasing returns, institutions do not matter. Institutional reforms, both political and economic, involve providing adaptive efficiency, which provides the incentives to encourage the development of decentralized decision making. Second, organizations are subject to path dependence, where history matters. Political and legal institutions can either facilitate or hinder the process of innovations and technology transfer. The fixed cost for any change to decentralized forms is very high, and it causes significant deviations from competitive efficiency. Finally, economic laws generate significant inefficiency due to lack of decentralization. Bureaucratic control and outdated laws of land reforms create stumbling blocks to incentive creation and dispersion. Some laws, which are progressive, are not adequately enforced. This creates more inefficiency in the developing countries. The NICs in Southeast Asia have been paying much attention to these aspects of reform of governance. Here also small countries such as Taiwan and Singapore have taken the lead. One measure of liberalization and policy reform has been used by Porter (2004) as a growth competitiveness index (GCI), which is based on three broad mechanisms: the macroeconomic environment (x_1), the quality of public institutions (x_2), and technology (x_3). These three are often called "the three pillars" of sustained economic growth. The following GCI (2003) rankings are illustrative:

	GCI rank			
	x_1	x_2	x_3	Total
USA	14	17	1	2
Taiwan	18	21	3	5
Singapore	1	6	12	6
China	25	52	65	44
India	52	55	64	56
Indonesia	64	76	78	72

Here higher values indicate lower competitive efficiency. The regression estimates reported by Porter saw that about 82% of the variation in GDP per capita across the sample of 101 countries is accounted for by the macroeconomic fundamentals (x_1). This shows the need for more transparency through the economic institutions such as banks, credit agencies, and stock markets.

Two important methods of achieving an efficient decentralization of decision system across the economy are how to reduce market distortions of all sorts, especially those related to government control, and how to develop market enhancing institutions and strategies. The case of China's economic policy reforms deserves special mention here. A World Bank study (1996) on the Chinese economy stressed the following key elements in China's growth during 1985–1994 when average

GDP growth was 10.2%. First, there were economic reforms comprising substantial liberalization of domestic prices, internal and international trade policies, and significant freedoms to agricultural households. This facilitated a gradual process of dissemination of best practice technology and incremental innovations. Second, large-scale reforms of state-owned enterprises were initiated by altering the policy environment, e.g., by reducing state subsidies and promoting competition through reducing barrier to entry and through increasing FDI. Entry into WTO has helped sustain the tempo of these reforms for China. Finally, a network of 18 cities (medium to large) has been selected under China's Ninth 5-year plan for comprehensive enterprise reform where additional capital was provided by the national government to augment production capacity, upgrade technology, and conduct more than 2,600 retraining programs for increasing the human skills.

Taiwan achieved significant success in its decentralization policy through technology diffusion. This has made it possible to sustain economic growth without increasing the inequality in income distribution. Both China and Taiwan realized very early that there exists a broad range of institutions at local and suburban areas that are complementary to the R&D activities in the IT sector. They attempted to utilize this linkage fully. For example one major source of linkage of IT sector growth with the growth of other complementary sectors is "the cluster effect," which generates large economies of scale and scope, e.g., the Silicon Valley and its link with Stanford University.

Inefficiency of the existing institutional system can be measured by an index of corruption constructed by Porter for 80 countries in 2003. The following ranks are illustrative.

	Corruption rank	Technology rank
USA	17	1
Taiwan	19	3
Singapore	5	12
China	50	65
India	80	64
Thailand	45	39

Corruption here comprises lapse in enforcement, bribery, and lack of transparency in the enforcement of laws. Note that India's position is worse than that of China. Taiwan's rank in technology is very close to the USA and its corruption rank is very low. Clearly the Indian policy makers have to improve their record. Two large economic costs are generated by corruption, which causes lack of transparency. One is the transaction costs, which are added to production costs. These costs reduce the competitive advantage of Indian business competing in world markets. Second, there is the rent-seeking activity, which increases through corruption and bureaucratic systems of graft. The rent-seeking attitude reduces the efficiency and hinders the incentive to invest and compete. Some estimates have put these costs to account for about 8–10% of national GDP in India. The so-called black market and the parallel economy run by the corruption system have rarely been analyzed by the Indian economists, since it is very difficult to obtain relevant economic data.

9.5 Cost of Debt Crisis

The GCI index stresses the role of good macroeconomic policy in sustaining economic growth. The successful NICs in Asia laid great stress on maintaining good fiscal policy and macroeconomic stability, which is so essential for long-run economic growth. Since FDI is a large component for these Asian NICs, the external debt comprises a larger part of total national debt. The following figures by the World Bank in millions of US dollars are illustrative:

	1980	1990	2000	2006
East Asia	81.8	114.3	81.8	44.1
Latin America	201.8	279.7	178.5	101.7
South Asia	160.5	380.8	181.9	84.3
Sub-Saharan Africa	91.7	219.3	186.6	89.0

It is clear that unlike Latin America the successful NICs in Asia incurred much less external debt and that these external loans were utilized most productively by Taiwan, China, and South Korea in three ways: to reduce the costs of learning by doing, to augment domestic investment so that the country gains competitive advantage in export, and to import new technology so that future competitiveness would improve. In the case of Latin America the utilization of foreign loans was very inefficient, and it generated more inflationary pressures.

Two major costs arise in debt crisis. First, it causes a persistent imbalance in the current account. It reflects a failure of good economic policy by not adopting the necessary structural transformation of the economy to achieve greater industrialization and more effective diversification of the productive structure. The Latin-American countries followed the path of least resistance, using external debt to finance current consumption or military expenditure. As a result huge inflationary pressures were generated, which hindered the real growth rates. Second, the real cost of debt is reflected in falling rates of overall investment. Thus, in Argentina, Brazil, Mexico, and a number of African countries, real gross investment decreased substantially from 1980 to 1900, and this is indicative of the costs arising from the effects of the debt crisis. A World Bank Study (2002) estimated the effect of debt overhang on economic growth. It found that when the debt burden exceeded 160–170% of exports and 35–40% of GDP, the impact of debt on economic growth becomes negative.

Thus, it is clear that a sound policy of debt management and a balanced fiscal policy in the short and medium term are essential for sustaining high economic growth.

9.6 Challenge of Globalization

Globalization of technology and trade has come to stay. No country can avoid its challenge today. Global competition, new information technology, and incremental innovation are bound to spread all over the world. Its two challenges are very often discussed. One is the following question: can the successful growth experience of the NICs in Asia be repeated by other countries? The other question is to what extent planning and policy can reduce the structural costs of responding to globalization.

The answer to the first question is mostly negative. Each country is basically conditioned by its path dependence, its institutional history, and resource structure. Learning of course can increase productivity but history matters. However, the experiences can be learned, strategies can be adopted, and many of the costs and mistakes of the first movers may be avoided. The dichotomy between countries endowed with natural resources, e.g., the Sub-Saharan Africa, is only one factor that distinguishes the Asian NICs from the Sub-Saharan countries. Rapid growth in China, Korea, and Taiwan were made possible by political stability, land reform, infrastructure development, and incentives for market reform and learning by doing through FDI. However, the key components of their success included the supportive state policy and liberalization in several fronts so that economic efficiency can be achieved and sustained.

In today's world of technology and innovation-intensive production and trade, dynamic comparative advantage replaces the static framework, and under conditions of uncertainty there is no optimum allocation of resources under the dynamics of technology innovations. Hence, there is no set of scientifically determined optimum public policies for technological change in general. In this specific sense the days of national planning in terms of any fixed set of rules are fast becoming obsolete. To assume that the bureaucrats or their agents can predict the optimum pace of development of innovations and technology change and thereby develop an optimum economic policy is more fiction than fact. Discretionary policy and adaptive efficiency should provide the key goals.

Certain safeguards, however, need to be taken as a valid economic response to the challenge of today's globalization. First, the fast pace of global competition may have a significant impact on the domestic business undergoing creative destruction. The state policy needs to soften this process, so that the middle and the poor can stand the cost of the process. The Taiwanese model offers a very good example. Second, the investment in human capital and the incremental innovations should be emphasized very strongly in the state policies and their welfare perspective. This calls for a strong emphasis on the technical, scientific, and general education. Third, there should be a strong emphasis on institutional reform with transparency enforced in all economic spheres in banking and credit markets and political governance. This may appear as a tall order, but there exists no other way. Finally, one should stress that in the final analysis the key to economic growth is national productivity and economic efficiency. To increase productivity over time allocating resources optimally over time and transforming the economic and social institutions so as to reduce their transaction costs should be the goal followed by any country that aspires to achieve a steady rate of economic growth over time. This is the gist of the growth miracles that happened in the successful NICs in Asia. Next-tier miracles are yet to occur under conditions of dynamic comparative advantage. Learning by doing, renewable resource, and general-purpose technology have yet to play their dynamic roles more fully.

References

Aghion, P., & Howitt, P. (1992). A model of growth through creative destruction. *Econometrica, 60*, 323–351.

Anderson, E. S. (1994). *Evolutionary Economics: Post–Schumpeterian Contributions*. London: Pinter Publishers.

Antonelli, C. (1995). The diffusion of new information technologies and productivity growth. *Journal of Evolutionary Economies, 5*, 1–17.

Arrow, K. J. (1962). The economic implications of learning by doing. *Review of Economic Studies, 29*, 155–174.

Baumol, W. (2002). *The Free Market Innovation Machine*. Princeton: Princeton University Press.

Borensztein, E., & Lee, J. (1998). How does foreign direct investment affect economic growth. *Journal of International Economics, 45*, 115–135.

Bosworth, B., & Collins, S. (2003). *The empirics of growth: An update.* Working paper. Washington, DC: Brookings Institution.

Cellini, R., & Lambertini, L. (2009). Dynamic R&D with spillover. *Journal of Economic Dynamics and Control, 33*, 568–582.

Coase, R. (1937). The nature of the firm. *Economica, 4*, 386–405.

Coase, R. (1998). Recent research on the firm. *Economica, 65*, 325–339.

Cohen, W. M., & Levinthal, D. A. (1989). Innovation and learning: the two faces of R&D. *Economic Journal, 99*, 569–596.

D'Aveni, R. A. (1994). *Hypercompetition*. New York: Free Press.

Dosi, G. (1984). *Technical change and industrial transformation*. London: Macmillan.

Eliasson, G. (1988). Schumpeterian innovation, market structure and the stability of industrial development. In H. Hanusch (Ed.), *Evolutionary economics: Applications of Schumpeter's ideas*. New York: Cambridge University Press.

Feenstra, R., Madam, D., Yang, T., & Liang, C. (1997). *Testing endogenous growth in South Korea and Taiwan.* Working paper. Cambridge, MA: National Bureau of Economic Research.

Folster, S., & Trofimov, G. (1997). Industry evolution and R& externalities. *Journal of Economic Dynamics and Control, 21*, 1727–1748.

Grossman, G. M., & Helpman, E. (1991) *Innovation and Growth in the Global Economy*. Cambridge, MA: MIT Press.

Hausmann, R., & Rodrick, D. (2003). Economic development as self-discovery. *Journal of Development Economics, 72*, 603–633.

Hayami, Y., & Gogo, Y. (2005). *Development Economics*. New York: Oxford University Press.

Heertje, A. (1988). Schumpeter and technology change. In H. Hanusch (Ed.), *Evolutionary economics: Applications of Schumpeter's ideas*. New York: Cambridge University Press.

J. Sengupta, *Understanding Economic Growth: Modern Theory and Experience*,
DOI 10.1007/978-1-4419-8026-7, © Springer Science+Business Media, LLC 2011

Helpman, E. (2004). *The Mystery of Economic Growth.* Cambridge, MA: Harvard University Press.
Henderson, J., & Cockburn, R. (1996). The evolution of integrative capability. *Industrial and Corporate Change, 3*, 607–625.
Hobday, M. (1995). *Innovation in East Asia: The challenge to Japan.* Aldershot: Edward Elgar.
Howells, J. (1998). Innovation and technology transfer within multinational firms. In J. Michie & J. Grieve Smith (Eds.), *Globalization, growth and governance.* New York: Oxford University Press.
Huang, J., Otsuka, K., & Rozelle, S. (2006). China's rural economy and the path to a modern industrial state. In J. Chen & S. Yao (Eds.), *Globalization competition and growth in China.* London: Routledge.
Jones, C. (1995). R&D based models of economic growth. *Journal of Political Economy, 103*, 759–784.
Jones, C. I. (1995a). Time series tests ofendogenous growth models. *Quarterly Journal of Economics, 110*, 495–525.
Jones, C. I. (1995b). R&D models of economic growth. *Journal of Political Economy, 103*, 759–784.
Jones, C. I. (2002). *Introduction to Economic Growth.* New York: Norton.
Kim, J. (2002). Information technology and firm performance in Korea. In T. Ito & A. Rose (Eds.), *Growth and productivity in East Asia.* Chicago: University of Chicago Press.
Kuznets, S. (1955). Economic growth and income inequality. *American Economic Review, 45*, 1–28.
Laursen, K. (1999). The impact of technological opportunity on the dynamics of trade performance. *Structural Change and Economic Dynamics, 10*, 341–357.
Lo, C. (2007). *Understanding China's growth.* New York: Palgrave Macmillan.
Lucas, R. E. (1993). Making a miracle. *Econometrica, 61*, 251–272.
Mankiew, N., Romer, D., & Weil, D. (1992) A contribution to the empirics of growth. *Quarterly Journal of Economics, 107*, 407–437.
Metcalfe, J. (1994). Competition, evolution and the capital market. *Metroeconomica, 4*, 127–154.
Nachum, L. (2002). *International business in a world of increasing returns.* Working Paper No WP 224, University of Cambridge, UK.
Nelson, R., & Phelps, E. (1966). Investment in humans, technological diffusion and economic growth. *American Economic Review, 61*, 69–75.
Nelson, R., & Winter, S. (1982). *An evolutionary theory of economic change.* Cambridge, MA: Belknap.
North, D. C. (1990) *Institutions, Institutional Change and Economic Performance.* New York: Cambridge University Press.
Pasinetti, L., & Solow, R. M. (1994). *Long term Economic Growth.* New York: Cambridge University Press.
Piek, H. (1998). *Technology development in rural industries.* London: Thela.
Platteau, J. (2008). Recent research on organization theory. *Journal of Economic Behavior and Organizations, 29*, 280–312.
Porter, M. E. (1980). From competitive advantage to corporate strategy. *Harvard Business Review, 65*, 43–59.
Porter, M. E. (1990). *The Competitive Advantage of Nations.* New York: Free Press.
Prahalad, C. K., & Hamel, G. (1990). The core competence of the corporation. *Harvard Business Review, 66*, 79–91.
Prahalad, C. K., & Hamel, G. (1994). *Competing for the future.* Cambridge: Harvard Business School Press.
Qian, X., & Smyth, R. (2006). Growth accounting for the Chinese provinces 1990-2000: Incorporating human capital accumulation. *Journal of Chinese Economic and Business Studies, 4*, 21–38.
Richardson, G. B. (1975). *Information and Investment.* Oxford: Clarendon Press.
Rodrick, D. (1994). King Kong meets Godzilla: The World Bank and the East Asia miracle. In A. Fishlow, C. Gwin, S. Haggard, D. Rodrick, & R. Wade (Eds.), *Miracle or design:*

Lessons from the East Asian experience. Washington, DC: Overseas Development Council.
Romer, P. (1990). Endogenous technological change. *Journal of Political Economy, 98*, 71–102.
Romer, P. M. (1994). The origins of endogenous growth. *Journal of Economic Perspectives, 8*, 3–22.
Sachs, J., Varshney, A., & Bajpai, N. (Eds.). (1999). *India in the era of economic reforms*. New York: Oxford University Press.
Sanders, R., & Chen, Y. (2006). *Crossing which river and feeling which stones? China's transition to the new economy*. London: Routledge.
Schumpeter, J. (1947). *Capitalism Socialism and Democracy*. (2nd ed.). New York: Harper Brothers.
Sengupta, J. K. (2003). *New Efficiency Theory*. New York: Springer.
Sengupta, J. K. (2004). *Competition and Growth*. New York: Palgrave Macmillan.
Sengupta, J. K. (2005). *India's economic growth*. New York: Palgrave Macmillan.
Sengupta, J. K. (2007). *Dynamics of entry and market evolution*. New York: Palgrave Macmillan.
Sengupta, J. K., & Neogi, C. (2009). *India's New Economy*. New York: Palgrave Macmillan.
Sengupta, J. K. (2010). *Technology, innovations and growth*. New York: Palgrave Macmillan.
Sengupta, J. K., & Fanchon, P. (2009). *Efficiency Market Dynamics and Industry Growth*. New York: Palgrave Macmillan.
Sengupta, J. K., & Lin, B. (1993). Recent rural growth in China 1980-86. *International Review of Applied Economics, 7*, 177–196.
Sengupta, J. K., & Phillip, F. (2009). *Efficiency market dynamics and industry growth*. New York: Palgrave Macmillan.
Sengupta, J. K., & Sahoo, B. (2006). *Efficiency Models in Data Envelopment Analysis*. New York: Palgrave Macmillan.
Simon, H. (1991). *The theory of the firm revisited*. New York: Cambridge University Press.
Smith, J. M. (1982). *Evolution and the theory of genes*. Cambridge: Cambridge University Press.
Solow, R. M. (1956). A contribution to the theory of economic growth. *Quarterly Journal of Economics, 70*, 65–94.
Solow, R. M. (1957). Technical change and the aggregate production function. *Review of Economics and Statistics, 39*, 312–320.
Spence, M. (1984). Cost reduction, competition, and industry performance, *Econometrica 52*, 101–122.
Teece, D. (1986). Profiting from technological innovation: Implications for integration, collaboration, licensing and public policy. *Research Policy, 15*, 285–305.
United Nations. (2004). *Human development report 2004*. New York: UNDP Programme.
Wang, Y., & Yao, Y. (2003). Sources of China's economic growth 1952-1999: Incorporating human capital accumulation. *China Economic Review, 14*, 32–52.
Williamson, O. E. (1985). *The economic institutions of capitalism: Firms, markets and relational contracting*. New York: Free Press.
Winter, S. (1984). Schumpeterian competition in alternative technological regimes. *Journal of Economic Behavior and Organizations, 5*, 287–320.
Winter, S. G. (2008). Dynamic capability as a source of change. In A. Ebner & N. Beck (Eds.), *The institutions of the market: Organization, social systems and governance*. New York: Oxford University Press.
World Bank. (1996). *World Development Report*. Oxford: Oxford University Press.
World Bank. (2002). *World Development Report*. Oxford: Oxford University Press.
Wu, Y. (2008). *Productivity, efficiency and economic growth in China*. New York: Palgrave Macmillan.
Yao, S., Jiang, C., Feng, G., & Willenbockel, D. (2006). WTO challenges and efficiency of Chinese banks. In J. Chen & S. Yao (Eds.), *Globalization, competition and growth in China*. London: Routledge.
Zheng, P., Giorgioni, G., & Siler, P. (2006). The impact of FDI on economic growth in China's regions. In J. Chen & S. Yao (Eds.), *Globalization, competition and growth in China*. London: Routledge.

Index

FSC
www.fsc.org
MIX
Papier | Fördert
gute Waldnutzung
FSC® C083411

Kolibri 360 GmbH
Ferdinand-Jühlke-Straße 7
99095 Erfurt, Deutschland
produktsicherheit@kolibri360.de